The Great Riddle

*Wittgenstein and Nonsense,
Theology and Philosophy*

The Stanton Lectures 2014

Stephen Mulhall

OXFORD
UNIVERSITY PRESS

OXFORD
UNIVERSITY PRESS

Great Clarendon Street, Oxford, OX2 6DP,
United Kingdom

Oxford University Press is a department of the University of Oxford.
It furthers the University's objective of excellence in research, scholarship,
and education by publishing worldwide. Oxford is a registered trade mark of
Oxford University Press in the UK and in certain other countries

© Stephen Mulhall 2015

The moral rights of the author have been asserted

First Edition published in 2015
Impression: 1

Published in the United States of America by Oxford University Press
198 Madison Avenue, New York, NY 10016, United States of America

British Library Cataloguing in Publication Data
Data available

Library of Congress Control Number: 2015942539

ISBN 978-0-19-875532-6

Printed in Great Britain by
Clays Ltd, St Ives plc

Contents

Preface

It was a great honour to be invited to give the Stanton Lectures in the Philosophy of Religion in the Lent term of 2014. The invitation was also particularly well timed from my point of view; for it arrived soon after I had participated in the Aquinas Colloquium organized by Blackfriars in Oxford during 2012, which had brought to my attention for the first time the theological school or movement named 'Grammatical Thomism', and given me a real desire to understand it better, and in particular to understand the legitimacy of its claims to inherit Wittgenstein just as much as Aquinas. So I would like to take this opportunity to express my thanks to the organizers of the Colloquium, and in particular to David Burrell and Janet Soskice, who also participated in it, and were extremely generous in their response to my initial attempts to get Grammatical Thomism into focus. I now appreciate far more than I did then just how influential and much-admired David's work is by theologians whose judgement I respect; and I would be very pleased if these lectures not only bring his work to the attention of a wider philosophical audience, but remind theologians and philosophers of religion that lying behind his well-known writings on the monotheistic religions of the book, and on Aquinas, is a very powerful and distinctive conception of philosophy.

I would also like to thank the Electors to the Stanton Lectureship for providing me with the opportunity to take the further steps in my theological education that are recorded in the following pages. Eamon Duffy was the Chair of the Electors, and a genial host at the dinner following my first lecture: he, together with Sarah Coakley, Janet Soskice, Tim Crane, Catherine Pickstock, and Judy Lieu, also provided gracious introductions to each of the six lectures in the series. Despite my folly in choosing to deliver the lectures during a full teaching term at my home university, which sorely truncated the time I could spend in Cambridge outside the two hours involved in delivering the lectures themselves and answering questions from the audience, the Theology Faculty were extremely generous hosts; and various members of the Philosophy Faculty also exerted themselves to make me feel at home. Amongst the theologians, I would particularly like to thank once again Janet Soskice and Sarah Coakley, both of whom helped me with useful references and pertinent responses as the lectures unfolded; I am particularly in Sarah's debt, since she made the time to read and respond in very helpful ways to the initial drafts of the whole series. Amongst the philosophers, Tim Crane, Arif Ahmed, Michael Potter, and Nicholas Boyle were welcome faces among the regular audience members, and charitable in their responses to my peculiar ways of doing philosophy, and of trying to find fruitful guidance in this task from theological sources. I would also like to thank Peter Harland, the Theology Faculty's administrative officer, and his colleagues, who dealt efficiently and courteously with all the practical matters arising from my tenure as Stanton Lecturer.

Although each of the lectures has been revised, and in some cases significantly expanded, I have tried to retain the style and tone of their original mode of presentation. Amongst colleagues who have taken the time to read and respond to the text of my lectures outside the context of their delivery, or have otherwise helped me to pursue lines of thought or references related to them, I would particularly like to thank Cora Diamond, Judith Wolfe, Stanley Hauerwas, Brian Klug, David Burrell, Joshua Furnal, Martin Kusch, and Iain McPherson.

Lectures One and Two incorporate revised versions of portions of my essay 'Wittgenstein on Religious Belief', first published in O. Kuusela and M. McGinn (eds), *The Oxford Companion to Wittgenstein* (Oxford: Oxford University Press, 2012).

As with any and all of my academic duties, I could not have carried out the responsibilities associated with this lectureship, or effected the transformation of the lecture texts into a short book, without the domestic support of Alison Baker, and the willingness of our two children (Ellie and Matt) to go without access to the study (and its computer) for significant portions of far too many days.

Lecture One

Nonsense and Theology
Exhausting the Options?

The starting point of this series of lectures was the recent discovery on my part of an approach to the task of reflectively comprehending religious uses of language that goes, or went, by the name of 'Grammatical Thomism'. The idea that there might be fruitful points of contact, or even substantial areas of overlap, between Wittgenstein's grammatical investigations of mind and language and Thomas Aquinas' treatment of those same topics—call this 'Analytic Thomism'—had long been familiar to me, primarily through my familiarity with the work of Anthony Kenny and Herbert McCabe. What was new (and deeply intriguing) to me was the idea that a text such as the *Summa Theologiae* might be fruitfully interpreted as, or at least controlled from the outset by, a grammatical investigation of the nature and limits of (what McCabe would call) the human capacity to know and name God, and that McCabe's way of carrying out this mode of reading Aquinas formed part of a broader interpretative project to which the work of David Burrell and Fergus Kerr (to name but two theological companions) could be taken to contribute, with the groundbreaking work of Victor Preller as an acknowledged inspiration.

It is my understanding that this project is now generally regarded as being part of the history of theology rather than of its vital present—as very much a project of the 1960s and 1970s, when Wittgenstein's later writings were at their most influential, and appeared to hold out to philosophically minded theologians a sympathetic alternative to the settled hostility of logical positivism—despite the fact that those associated with it continued their work well beyond that period, and their basic orientation continues to receive occasional expressions of collective respect.[1] When I asked why the project had so quickly become passé, I was pointed towards Francesca Aran Murphy's book, *God is Not a Story*, according to which Grammatical Thomism evinces all the vices of Wittgensteinianism and none of the virtues of Thomas.[2] I found Murphy's way of prosecuting the first of these charges deeply unconvincing, for it depends not so much upon a reasoned rejection of a Wittgensteinian approach as a failure to appreciate the nature of that approach, and of the reasons its proponents have for adopting it; and since that misunderstanding continues to be broadly shared (not only within the philosophy of religion), it may be worth taking a few moments at the outset to address it.

Murphy's critique of Grammatical Thomism appears to depend upon a single idea, which then appears in a number of variations according to the particular Grammatical Thomist text and author under critical discussion—namely, that they all offer 'a theory aimed at translating metaphysical concerns [about God's being] into concerns about the logic of religious language' (GNS, 89). This guiding characterization presupposes that concerns about the metaphysical essence of God and concerns about the grammar of religious language are not only fundamentally different but also contrasting or contradictory: according to Murphy, if someone is analysing or otherwise reflecting upon our talk about God, then she is not reflecting upon God's nature or essence. From which it follows that to translate reflections of the latter kind into reflections of the former kind (or to interpret the latter kind of enterprise in terms of the former) is not only to misrepresent genuinely metaphysical reflection; it is to eviscerate or etiolate it, by reducing a concern for the ultimate ground of being to an anthropocentric, reflexive, and emptily formal reflection on our means of representing reality rather than on the reality we aspire to represent.

For Wittgenstein, however, elucidating grammar and articulating the essence of things are not distinct tasks at all. On the contrary: according to his later writings, '*Essence* is expressed in grammar . . . Grammar tells

---

[1]   As in J. Stout and R. MacSwain (eds), *Grammar and Grace: Reformulations of Aquinas and Wittgenstein* (London: SCM Press, 1984)—a volume dedicated to the memory of Victor Preller and his *Divine Science and the Science of God: A Reformulation of Thomas Aquinas* (Princeton, NJ: Princeton University Press, 1967).

[2]   Oxford: Oxford University Press, 2007, hereafter 'GNS'.

what kind of object anything is (Theology as grammar).' (PI,[3] 371, 373.)
A philosopher is characteristically interested in the essence of things—
not the facts of nature but rather the basis or essence of everything
empirical, the space of possibilities within which what happens to be
the case locates itself. But Wittgenstein suggests that essence finds
expression in the kinds of statement that we make about the relevant
phenomenon. What it does (or does not) make sense to say about
something makes manifest its essential possibilities, the kinds of features
it must possess if it is to count as the kind of thing it is, as well as the
kinds of variation of feature to which it might intelligibly be subject
without ceasing to count as that kind of thing. Hence, philosophical
inquiries into essence—call this metaphysics—can and must take the
form of grammatical investigations; the essence of things can be rendered surveyable simply by a rearrangement of what any speaker already
knows—how to use words, what to say when.

Might not the thing's essence nevertheless differ from our concept of
it, so that its true, underlying nature is not manifest in, but rather hidden
by, the grammar of our discourse about it? But grammar could only be a
false or otherwise misleading representation of what is really the case if it
is in the business of representing reality in the first place; and it is not.
Grammar articulates the terms in which a given kind of thing can
intelligibly be represented (truly or falsely). But if one regards those
terms as themselves representations of something, one is attempting to
conceive of a mode of discourse as if it were a particular discursive act—
as if grammar itself were a deployment of grammar, and clarifications of
meaning were descriptions of reality. It amounts to viewing the distinction between sense and nonsense as if it were a species of the distinction
between truth and falsehood; and that view embodies a misunderstanding that will profoundly distort one's metaphysical aspirations, in the
absence of a grammatical elucidation of the relevant distinctions
(between sense and truth, definitions and descriptions, representations
and their enabling conditions).

This is one familiar way of recounting the grammar of Wittgenstein's
concept of 'grammar'; and of course, simply recounting it does not
amount to demonstrating that the highly controversial conception of

---

[3] *Philosophical Investigations*, 4th edition, trans. Anscombe, Hacker, and Schulte, ed.
Hacker and Schulte (Oxford: Blackwell, 2009), hereafter PI.

philosophy it engenders is right. But it does at least make clear that any genuinely Wittgensteinian Thomist enterprise will not only reject Murphy's conception of metaphysical and grammatical investigations as distinct or even contradictory, together with her privileging of metaphysics over what she takes to be explorations of mere words; it will do so for reasons having to do with a certain, well worked-out conception of the intimacy of the relation between the grammar of a language and reality. Since that fundamental methodological disagreement is never properly identified or engaged with at any point in Murphy's book, her criticisms of the Grammatical Thomists will seem to them—as they seem to me—to fail even to locate their intended target.

Even if one dismisses Murphy's attribution of Wittgensteinian vice to the Grammatical Thomists, however, that still leaves unaddressed her second charge—that Grammatical Thomists lack the virtues of any genuinely Thomistic theology. I certainly would not deny that one legitimate theological ground for dismissing Grammatical Thomism would be a lack of conviction in it as a plausible reading of Thomas Aquinas (and of his *Summa* in particular)—an exegetical matter about which I am very much not competent to adjudicate. As a philosopher, however, I am constitutionally inclined to be as much interested in possibilities as in actualities, and so to evaluate Grammatical Thomism as one way in which a Christian theological enterprise might be coherently and fruitfully conducted (whether or not its putative progenitor ever did so conduct it). And as a philosopher for whom the later work of Wittgenstein has been deeply influential from my undergraduate days, I am particularly interested in whether this possible mode of doing theology genuinely exhibits the indebtedness to Wittgenstein to which its name also lays claim. Indeed, one way of characterizing the core concern of this lecture series taken as a whole is as an attempt to show that, however things may be with the Grammatical Thomist claim to inherit Aquinas, its claim to inherit Wittgenstein is both well grounded and—once those grounds are properly appreciated—such as to justify the belief that it ought to be a serious contender in contemporary debates in theology and the philosophy of religion.

Such a positive evaluation of the grammaticality of Grammatical Thomism is, however, likely to encounter as much opposition from informed Wittgensteinian philosophers as its claim to be a valid reading of Aquinas has (it appears) encountered amongst Thomist theologians.

For as I began to read each individual Grammatical Thomist's body of work more systematically, and more systematically in relation to their theological brethren, it became clear that one central point of resemblance between them lay in their willingness to characterize discourse about God as nonsensical—more specifically, their willingness to take as a touchstone of theological insight the awareness that language was essentially incapable of putting us in touch with the reality of God, given the fact that (as mainstream Christianity has always averred) he is utterly transcendent with respect to the world we users of language inhabit, and in relation to which our words attain and maintain whatever meaning or sense they possess.

'Nonsense' is of course a pivotal term in Wittgenstein's philosophy, both early and late. For throughout his intellectual career he claimed that the 'problems' characteristic of philosophy, to which its metaphysical theory-building was intended to provide solutions, were in fact confusions resulting from a misunderstanding of the logic of our language: they signalled points at which speakers had lost control of their words, failing to mean anything at all just when they believed themselves to be communicating insights into the essence of reality.

To be sure, on the standard reading of the *Tractatus Logico-Philosophicus*,[4] Wittgenstein there allowed that certain kinds of violation of the limits of sense were nevertheless ways of gesturing towards ineffable insights; and the relevant kinds of strictly nonsensical utterance centrally included evaluative propositions (both aesthetic, and ethico-religious—what Wittgenstein called 'the mystical')—as well as the philosophical propositions that made up the *Tractatus* itself (since they attempted to delineate that which could not be otherwise—the essence of language—and so could not be articulated in propositions whose meaningfulness was supposed to depend upon their depicting a possible state of affairs, hence one that precisely could have been otherwise). But on the standard reading of Wittgenstein's later philosophy, that idea of ineffably insightful nonsense has been jettisoned altogether; hence it comes naturally to certain Wittgensteinians to think that, insofar as religion's search for the transcendent pushes human discourse beyond the limits of intelligibility, it results in sheer nonsense—the mere absence

[4] London: Routledge and Kegan Paul, 1922.

of sense. On the other hand, the later Wittgenstein also claimed that philosophy has no authority to subvert or reform our ordinary ways with words, but must rather seek simply to describe them—that our forms of life with language must ultimately be accepted; hence it comes naturally to certain other Wittgensteinians to think that, insofar as religious language-games are played, then religious forms of life are immune to philosophical critique in general, and in particular to the charge of lacking sense. This position is often described as one of Wittgensteinian fideism (much to the chagrin of its proponents).

A recent example of the former way of inheriting the later Wittgenstein is Bede Rundle's book, *Why there is Something rather than Nothing*,[5] in which he argues that a creator of the material world is not required, since there is no alternative to its existence. In the course of constructing that intriguing and sophisticated argument, he offers a range of additional (and in my view rather less sophisticated) reasons for questioning the coherence of traditional theism, all of which ultimately turn on the Wittgensteinian vision of language and the conditions under which it has sense that are outlined in his opening chapter, and that are crystallized in the following passage:

Someone who insists that God, though lacking eyes and ears, watches him incessantly and listens to his prayers, is clearly not using 'watch' or 'listen' in a sense we can recognize, so while the words may be individually meaningful and their combination grammatical, that is as far as meaningfulness goes: what we have is an unintelligible use of an intelligible form of words. God is not of this world, but that is not going to stop us speaking of him as if he were. It is not that we have a proposition which is meaningless because unverifiable, but we simply misuse the language, making an affirmation which, in the light of our understanding of the words, is totally unwarranted, an affirmation that makes no intelligible contact with reality. (WSN, 11)

In the light of my current concern, it is striking that Rundle goes on immediately to cite John Haldane's rendition of a basic Thomist claim about God (that 'if there is a God identified initially as a first cause, then *that* he is and *what* he is are one and the same reality') as a theological pronouncement so incoherent that it defies even grammar:

[T]he different ways in which the phrases 'that God is' and 'what God is' may be completed show that any talk of the same reality is incoherent. That God is can be

---

[5] Oxford: Oxford University Press, 2004, hereafter 'WSN'.

said to be true, but not what God is, whereas 'What God is is benevolent' makes sense, but not 'That God is is benevolent'. (WSN, 11)

Here, Rundle echoes one criticism advanced in a much earlier Wittgen-steinian critique of Aquinas (influential at least in philosophy, if not theology)—Anthony Kenny's *The Five Ways*.[6] Kenny ends his discussion of the Fourth Way by savaging this same Thomist claim:

Aquinas, in order to prevent God's *esse* from being the applicability of a quite uninformative predicate [because invoking an attribute common to anything possessing substantial or accidental form], turns it into the applicability of a predicate which is no predicate at all. What he says comes to this. When we say, of anything but God, that it IS, we mean that for some F . . . it is F; when we say of God that he IS, we mean the same except that no predicate may be substituted for the F which occurs in the formula. God isn't anything of any kind, he just is. But this is surely complete nonsense. For the only meaning that attaches to a formula such as 'God is F' is that if you substitute a genuine predicate for the dummy letter F, you will get a meaningful sentence. If you forbid such a substitution, you must delete the variable letter . . . and you are left simply with 'God is . . . ' which . . . is just an incomplete sentence.

The notion of *Ipsum Esse Subsistens*, therefore, so far from being a profound metaphysical analysis of the divine nature, turns out to be the Platonic Idea of a predicate which is at best uninformative and at worst unintelligible. (FW, 94–5)

Even those sympathetic to Wittgenstein might feel that both Kenny and Rundle are remarkably quick to assume that the challenges to intelligibility to which they point have simply been missed not only by those inclined to employ them but also by those whose theological employment it is to reflect upon such uses, and remarkably reluctant to imagine why any intelligent person might nevertheless find some point or purpose in such uses of words. If, however, one *is* sympathetic to Wittgensteinian modes of doing philosophy, and in particular to his methodological injunction against philosophical attempts to interfere with our ordinary forms of life with language, one will have an additional incentive to resist the admittedly powerful initial impression of sheer nonsensicality that religious uses of language so persistently create, and instead explore the possibility that this impression is indeed the result of a failure to see the true nature of the mode of employment of words that

---

[6] London: Routledge and Kegan Paul, 1969, hereafter 'FW'.

is at issue—a misperception of the actual grammar of the language-games being played here.

The work of D.Z. Phillips is perhaps the most sustained philosophical attempt to provide an accurate delineation of the grammar of religious language in this vein—the second (and by far the most influential) of the two ways of inheriting the later Wittgenstein that I distinguished earlier. And in doing so, he confronts perhaps its most difficult challenge, by acknowledging the persistence with which Biblical texts and protagonists emphasize that God and his ways are beyond human understanding—as when St Paul exclaims 'how unsearchable are his judgements, and his ways past finding out' (Rom. 11:33), or the Psalmist says that God's 'knowledge is too wonderful for me; it is high, I cannot attain unto it' (139:6). Phillips admits that it is tempting to gloss such texts as claiming that human language is inherently inadequate to God's nature and ways; but he urges us not to succumb, because that claim is not obviously comprehensible:

> To say that language as such is inherently adequate or inadequate requires finding sense in the idea of a complete language, such that looking at its completeness (all that can ever be said), we can say that it, this complete language, is either adequate or inadequate. Since the notion of completeness is unintelligible, talk of the adequacy or inadequacy of a complete language is also unintelligible. (FF,[7] 263)

But such a gloss on these words is not compulsory—it is, indeed, indicative of a significant misunderstanding:

> The first thing it is essential to note is that . . . the Psalmist and St. Paul are not making statements *about* human language. Their expressions of religious mystery are expressions *in* language. They are not telling us that, because of the inadequacy of language, they cannot praise God. Praising God is precisely what they are doing! . . . [They] are not telling us that God is hidden from them because of the inadequacy of their language. Rather, they are showing us that the notion of God, *in* their language, is that of a hidden God: 'Verily thou are a God that hidest thyself, O God of Israel, the Saviour' [Isaiah 45:15]. (FF, 278–9)

In other words, 'mystery'—like any other religious concept—is a concept that is used by religious believers; so the philosopher interested in understanding the role of mystery in religion need only delineate the

---

[7] *Faith after Foundationalism* (London: Routledge, 1989).

place that expressions such as 'God's ways are beyond human under-standing' actually have in the human forms of life which employ them. More precisely, 'he must show the relation between such talk and facts concerning the limits of human existence, ragged facts, which must not be tidied up' (WR,[8] 166). The facts Phillips has in mind are the blind forces of nature, the transitoriness of fame, the unpredictable visitations of disease and death: and religious believers respond to them in a particular way—as:

things come from God's hands, the God who sends rain on the just and the unjust... Everything is ours by the grace of God... nothing is ours by right... The natural world, and other people, are seen as God's gifts, not to be appropri-ated through domination by us. To think otherwise is to fail to die to the self, to play at being God. (WR, 166-7)

On Phillips' view, such reactions are not compulsory: where one person speaks of God's gifts, another may speak of luck, and a third of absurdity. But those who speak in such ways are far closer to one another than they are to those who seek to explain or explain away these facts (whether by theodicy or science), because the former recognize that these limits are the point at which explanation, and so understanding, runs out. When such experiences elicit the question 'Why?', the questioner does not really seek an answer, but rather reactions or responses which replace the question; and the religious response is to seek to die to the desire for answers, for an explanation. In other words, for Phillips, 'when [believ-ers] speak of that which passes understanding, they invite us to consider the possibility of reacting to human life in a way other than by the understanding' (WR, 149).

Phillips' refusal to saddle religious believers with the idea that God's ways are mysterious because we are trapped within merely human limitations of reason and sense-making is admirable; so too is his recognition that if we are to grasp the significance of talk of divine transcendence, we must grasp its role in the life of those who employ it. But illuminating though his remarks on that role may be, if they were regarded as exhausting the function of such talk, then they risk leaving us with a strikingly comprehensible account of God's mysterious ways. After all, the forces of nature and the unpredictable visitations of death

---

[8] Phillips, D.Z., *Wittgenstein and Religion* (London: Routledge, 1993), hereafter 'WR',

and disease that Phillips cites as conditioning our use of the concept of 'mystery' seem perfectly unmysterious features of human life; and by claiming that this concept marks the point at which life should not be regarded as posing a challenge to our understanding at all (or at most the challenge of recognizing the irrelevance of understanding), he so successfully demystifies the notion of 'mystery' that he also threatens to denature it.

More importantly, when Phillips rather dismissively says that St Paul's and the Psalmist's talk about religious mystery are expressions in language rather than statements about language, he seems to forget the possibility that they might be both. It's as if he believes that, since talk about God's mysteriousness is a kind of talk, then it can't (on pain of patent self-contradiction, and so the imputation of extreme stupidity to those employing them) centrally include denials that words can be used intelligibly to talk about God; so those apparent denials must be understood otherwise—indeed, as having to do with something other than the understanding. Whereas, in truth, since any religious utterances that did concern the inherent powers of language in relation to divinity must *ex hypothesi* be linguistic utterances, it can hardly constitute an objection to taking St Paul's or the Psalmist's words as statements about language to point out that they are expressed in language.

It is surely undeniable that, in the history of Christianity, theologians reflecting on the nature and legitimacy of their community's religious discourse have persistently seen such ways of talking about God as having troubling implications for our understanding how any and all meaningful talk about God is possible. Phillips assumes that anyone who takes this to be a genuine difficulty is committed to the unintelligible notion of an absolutely complete language, one containing all that can ever conceivably be said, and concludes that we must therefore gloss the notion of religious mystery in terms other than those pertaining to language and understanding. But even if we accept that this notion is unintelligible, and further accept (*pace* Kenny and Rundle) that this does not simply provide further evidence of the inherent dependence of religion upon nonsense, we might still deny that theologians can only articulate a sense of God's transcendence of our language by invoking the notion of an absolutely complete language. They might, for example, do so by denying that any actual or conceivable forms of religious language (of the familiar concrete, finite, sort) could possibly be adequate to God's reality.

This suggestion needs, and will later receive, much more elucidation; and of course this aspect of Phillips' work deserves a much more extensive discussion than I have so far given it. But it will prove helpful at later stages of my argument about Grammatical Thomism if I continue our examination of this second way of inheriting Wittgenstein for the philosophy of religion by shifting its focus to an exemplary (even a notorious) paper by Wittgenstein's student and friend, Norman Malcolm, entitled 'Anselm's Ontological Arguments'.[9]

Malcolm distinguishes two different ontological arguments in Anselm's *Proslogion*: one which presupposes that existence is a perfection, and another which presupposes that necessary existence is a perfection. Malcolm concurs with the general opinion that Kant's critique decisively refutes the first of these arguments, but he denies that it refutes the second; for whereas it seems evident that 'existence' cannot be regarded (logically or grammatically speaking) as greater or more perfect than 'non-existence', the same is not true of 'necessary existence' when compared with 'contingent existence'. On the contrary: Malcolm claims that there are straightforward grammatical connections in ordinary language between the ideas of contingent existence, dependency, limitation, and imperfection, and hence between the idea of a perfect being—that than which nothing greater can be conceived—and non-contingent or necessary existence.

A being whose existence is contingent is one that might not have existed; hence its actual existence must have an explanation—it must in some way be dependent upon the existence and/or actions of something else. A computer that requires a mains electricity source if it is to function can intelligibly be said to be less great or more limited, hence less perfect, than one that does not; hence, any being whose existence is dependent upon something outside itself could not intelligibly be said to be a perfect being, for it would then be possible to imagine something greater or more perfect than it (namely, something which lacked that dependency or limitation). Since the Christian tradition conceives of God precisely as 'that than which nothing greater can be conceived', it follows that God's existence must be non-dependent, non-contingent—that is, necessary.

---

[9] *Philosophical Review* 69: 1960, reprinted in his *Knowledge and Certainty* (Englewood Cliffs, NJ: Prentice-Hall, 1963), to which all references to this article, hereafter AOA, will be keyed.

But unless the very idea of a necessarily existent being is incoherent, then its existence cannot be an open (that is, a contingent) question: its non-existence is simply inconceivable.

On Malcolm's view, this idea of God's necessary existence must be accurately articulated before the question of its coherence can be assessed. It certainly cannot be adequately captured in the following formulation, so popular with Kantians: if God exists, then he exists necessarily. For the antecedent clause takes away what the consequent clause appears to allow, presenting what it acknowledges is a necessity as if it were really a contingency; it amounts to a form of words which subverts its apparent sense, and thus necessarily fails to be about what it professes to be about. Insofar as it conceives of its subject matter as something whose existence is a contingent matter, then whatever it purports to pick out cannot be whatever the concept 'God' picks out. In Wittgensteinian terms, such a formulation embodies an incoherent attempt to speak simultaneously from within and without the relevant religious language-game; its internal invocation of necessity attempts to acknowledge the actual meaning of the religious believer's words, but its overarching commitment to contingency in fact gives expression to an outsider's incomprehension of that meaning. In terms closer to An-selm's: insofar as the atheist's denial of God's existence takes a form which implies that what he claims does not exist might conceivably have done so, then what he denies is not and cannot be what the believer affirms when she says that God exists. Such an atheism is fated to miss its target; it is not false, but inherently foolish—the expression of a concep-tual confusion.

But can the very idea of necessary existence, and so of God's necessary existence, be coherent? Must not all genuinely existential propositions be synthetic or contingent? Malcolm counters this suspicion by comparing the proposition 'God necessarily exists' with the Euclidean theorem 'There are an infinite number of prime numbers.' For if we can say that the latter asserts the existence of something *in some sense*, then we can surely say the same of the former. What we need to understand in each case is the particular sense of the proposition, more specifically the differences between such ways of talking of existence and the ways in which we talk of it in empirical contexts (which of course might them-selves be various, e.g. 'There is a low pressure area over the Great Lakes' as opposed to 'He still has a pain in his abdomen'). In short, '[t]here are as many kinds of existential propositions as there are kinds of subjects of discourse' (AOA, 153).

Malcolm imagines a Kantian who argues that whenever I think of a being as supremely or perfectly real, even as the supreme reality, the question surely still remains whether it exists or not; then he asks whether we would say the same in response to Euclid's demonstration of the existence of an infinity of primes. In the face of a proof of this theorem, it would surely not remain an open question whether or not there is an infinity of primes. Why, then, can we not say that, once Anselm has demonstrated the necessary existence of a being greater than which cannot be conceived, no question can then remain as to whether it exists or not? If we understand the kind of proof with which Euclid presents us, we understand the sense in which there is an infinity of primes; and likewise, insofar as we understand the proof with which Anselm presents us, we understand the sense in which there is a God— the sense in which he exists necessarily.

Nevertheless, to clarify the specifically religious sense of the idea of necessary existence, we must ultimately depart from our comparison with mathematics, and focus on its distinctively religious employment. Here, Malcolm cites Psalm 90: 'before the mountains were brought forth, or ever thou hadst formed the earth and the world, even from everlasting to everlasting, thou art God'. He comments:

Here is expressed the idea of the necessary existence and eternity of God, an idea that is essential to the Jewish and Christian religions. In those complex systems of thought, those 'language-games', God has the status of a necessary being. Who can doubt that? Here we must say with Wittgenstein, 'This language-game is played!' I believe we may rightly take the existence of those religious systems of thought in which God figures as a necessary being to be a disproof of the dogma . . . that no existential proposition can be necessary. (AOA, 156)

Even if we accept the coherence of the notion of God's necessary existence, however, Malcolm accepts that questions would still remain about its significance—its point or purpose. As he puts it, how can the concept have any meaning for anyone? Why should human beings even form such a concept, let alone participate in the forms of religious life surrounding it? If we cannot answer such questions, Malcolm thinks, then our admittedly coherent concept of God as a necessary being will nonetheless appear to be an 'arbitrary and absurd construction' (AOA, 161). His own answer is that the concept arises from recognizable experiential phenomena of human life, certain kinds of psychological (more precisely, emotional) responses to its vicissitudes. His primary example is that of guilt—a guilt so great that one is sure that nothing one could do oneself, nor any forgiveness offered by another human being, would remove it: a guilt greater than which cannot be conceived. 'Out of such a storm in the soul, I am suggesting, there arises the conception of a forgiving mercy that is limitless, beyond all measure' (AOA, 160).

What, then, should we conclude about the relation of Anselm's argument to religious belief? Does it show that believing in God is rationally required of us? The whole thrust of Malcolm's paper thus far has been to suggest that Anselm's argument is indeed a deductively valid proof of God's (necessary) existence; but in its final paragraph, Malcolm declares that he

can imagine an atheist going through the argument, becoming convinced of its validity, acutely defending it against objections, yet remaining an atheist. The only effect it could have on the fool of the Psalm would be that he stopped saying in his heart 'There is no God', because he would now realize that this is something he cannot meaningfully say or think. It is hardly to be expected that a demonstrative argument should, in addition, produce in him a living faith. (AOA, 161)

The religious value of the argument is thus, in the first instance, negative— it may remove some misplaced scruples about faith; but it would be unreasonable to require that recognizing Anselm's demonstration as valid must produce a conversion. Indeed, Malcolm suggests, Anselm's argument 'can be thoroughly understood only by one who has a view of that human "form of life" that gives rise to the idea of an infinitely great being, who views it from the *inside* not just from the outside and who has, therefore, at least some inclination to *partake* in that religious form of life' (AOA, 162). The relevant inclination here derives, Malcolm says, from the emotions—the very human phenomena that prompt the construction and inform the deployment of the concept that the proof aims to support. And Malcolm concludes by asserting that this inclination is not an effect of Anselm's argument, but is rather presupposed in the fullest understanding of it.

If one thinks of the argument of Malcolm's paper as exemplary of what I have called the second way of inheriting the later Wittgenstein, then it is not difficult to see why Wittgensteinian philosophy of religion conducted in this vein has been charged with amounting to a philosophically untenable version of fideism. I have gone into Malcolm's argument in such detail because I want to show both why it might appear to invite such a charge, and why it in fact does not merit attack on these grounds. Only when this is made clear will it be possible to see grounds for concern about Malcolm's approach, and so about the way of inheriting Wittgenstein that it exemplifies, and that are at once better anchored in his text and more directly pertinent to my engagement with Grammatical Thomism.

In the fateful article which first advanced this criticism, Kai Nielsen specified the unacceptable core of Wittgensteinian fideism as follows:

There is no Archimedean point in terms of which a philosopher (or for that matter anyone else) can relevantly criticize whole modes of discourse or, what comes to the same thing, ways of life, for each mode of discourse has its own specific criteria of rationality/irrationality, intelligibility/unintelligibility and reality/unreality. (WF,[10] 22)

The final paragraph of Malcolm's paper certainly serves sharply to differentiate the proper functioning of Anselm's proof from that of Euclid's, and so presumably the notion of proof in religious contexts from the same notion in mathematical contexts. For someone who grasped the deductive validity of Euclid's demonstration of his theorem about prime numbers could hardly reject its existential implications throughout number theory and beyond; whereas Malcolm appears to accept such a diremption in the religious case. And this hangs together with Malcolm's general insistence on the need to distinguish religious senses of terms from their sense in other contexts. Plainly, such a pervasive emphasis on the logical distinctness of various modes of discourse lies at the root of Nielsen's sense that Wittgensteinians picture our life with language as falling apart (at least analytically) into self-sufficient linguistic compartments or subsystems.

Moreover, Malcolm's distinction between appreciating Anselm's argument as a piece of logic, and appreciating its fullest or deepest religious significance, looks like an instance of a more general distinction between the deliverances of reason and the deliverances of faith; and then the core dogma of fideism will seem certainly to be in the offing (particularly when Malcolm explicitly links his line of thought with Kierkegaard's

---

[10] 'Wittgensteinian Fideism', *Philosophy* 42: 1967, reprinted in K. Nielsen and D.Z. Phillips (eds), *Wittgensteinian Fideism* (London: SCM Press, 2005), to which these page references are keyed.

claim that 'There is only one proof of the truth of Christianity and that . . . is from the emotions'[11]). For what at first seems to be an exposition of a deductively valid rational argument for religious belief turns out in the end to articulate a chain of reasoning that can only be properly understood, let alone endorsed, from the perspective of faith. And Malcolm invites further trouble by associating his first distinction with another—that between viewing religion from the outside and viewing it from the inside—and linking the latter with the perspective of a participant in religious forms of life. It is not hard to see why Nielsen might read this as an invitation to conclude that the significance of religious concepts can only be grasped by religious believers.

In truth, however, all of these apparent difficulties with Malcolm's position can be significantly eased. First, his insistence on the variety of kinds of existential proposition is in fact counterbalanced (however infrequently) by an acknowledgement of logical connections between the relevant modes of discourse, insofar as each has its place in the unifying context of the human form of life. After all, Malcolm does insist that the religious idea of divine perfection has its grammatical counterpart, and perhaps even its origins, in empirical contexts, when the various dependencies and limitations of material objects and instruments are under evaluation. And his concluding attempt to show that religious concepts are not only coherent but also possessed of sense and point depends precisely upon underlining their relation to elements in the common fabric of human experience.

Second, Malcolm's pivotal distinction between appreciating the logical validity of the argument and appreciating its religious significance is *not* a distinction between no understanding and genuine understanding: it is a distinction between one level of understanding and another, deeper or fuller level. The atheist who grasps the validity of Anselm's argument does indeed grasp one aspect of the grammar of the concept of God as it is employed in the Judaeo-Christian tradition, and hence must (on Malcolm's understanding of the significance of grammar) to that extent grasp the meaning of that concept. What he lacks is the deepest or fullest understanding of it—a grasp of what he calls 'the *sense* of the concept' (AOA, 161), by which I take him to mean the point or purpose of using

---

[11]   *The Journals*, ed. A. Dru (Oxford: Oxford University Press, 1938), section 926.

it, which in turn he associates with an appreciation of the view of human life that it serves to articulate. And Malcolm never says that this deeper understanding is available only to participants in religious forms of life; he claims rather that only those who have at least some inclination to partake in such forms of life can attain it. One might well have such an inclination without ever acting upon it: one might not only understand that some human beings can suffer guilt of a kind greater than which cannot be conceived, but actually suffer it oneself, without coming to believe that there is a source of forgiveness commensurate with it. If so, then in principle, both levels or aspects of a genuine understanding of religious concepts, proofs, and practices are attainable by those who are not practising believers, hence by at least one subset or category of atheists.

Even if one accepts these defences, however, real difficulties remain; and these difficulties are not only worth taking seriously from a Wittgensteinian perspective, but also turn out to have a particular bearing on my current concern with Grammatical Thomism. In particular, if it is so important to a deeper understanding of Anselm's argument and the concept it supports to appreciate the specific sense, the distinctive point or purpose, of their religious uses, then Malcolm's article does far less to encourage that deeper understanding than it initially appears to do. I don't just mean that his invocation of unforgivable guilt and despair are merely gestures towards an account of the point of religious concepts (although they are, as Malcolm recognizes); one cannot, after all, do everything in one journal article. I also mean that Malcolm's general manner of elucidating Anselm's argument about God—by comparing it with other, non-religious modes of discourse on existence and necessity—creates the appearance of generating a genuinely substantial or positive account of the grammar of religious discourse only by implicitly exploiting lines of continuity between religious and non-religious uses of words that it must then officially deny.

For example, Malcolm repeatedly emphasizes that the religious sense of claims about God's existence should be sharply distinguished from empirical existential claims; but his account of Anselm's argument attempts to clarify the grammatical link in religious discourse between God's perfection and his necessary existence primarily by invoking a chain of grammatical links (between imperfection, dependence, and limitation, on the one hand, and perfection, independence, and absence of limitation on the other) which have their home in empirical contexts. In illustrating these links, I talked of computers, whereas Malcolm talks of dishes and engines, but all concern beings of a kind with which—on Malcolm's official line—God must be contrasted rather than compared. A less limited or dependent empirical object might well be said to be more perfect or greater than its more limited counterparts, but it could never entirely lack the very possibility of limitation, which is internal to Anselm's characterization of God. In other words, the relevant comparisons succeed only in giving us a clear picture of a familiar way of talking about the existence of things that is not an intelligible way of talking about God's existence, which does not amount to giving us any insight at all into how we can intelligibly talk about God. Propositions such as 'God's existence is necessary' are thereby given or shown to have a use in warding off mistaken or irreligious talk of God as if he were a being amongst beings; but they do not actually tell us what Malcolm seems to think they tell us—namely, what genuinely religious talk of God (talk that is properly directed to its target) might amount to.

Similarly, although Malcolm points to mathematical talk of necessary existence primarily as a way of blocking the suggestion that religious talk of necessary existence is illegitimate because *any* talk of necessary existence is illegitimate, it is far from clear that he properly acknowledges that such talk of necessity has a different sense in these two different contexts. Invoking Psalm 90 certainly allows him to point out that religious believers connect the idea of God's necessary existence with the idea that he is eternal; but his only specification of what God's eternity might amount to consists in pointing out that the notion excludes all sentences implying that God has duration, even endless duration (AOA, 148)—a point which, even if true, fails to distinguish God in this respect from numbers, in relation to which talk of duration is surely equally excluded.

It's as if Malcolm is saying: you can be confident that religious uses of the concepts of perfection, non-dependence, and necessary existence are intelligible because there are intelligible non-religious uses of all those concepts; the religious concepts are just like those non-religious uses, only different—distinctively religious, but equally viable. A charitable reader of Malcolm's paper might say that the absence or gap where a positive grammatical account of religious language-games ought to be is only contingent, not necessary; indeed, he might go further and say that the paper itself contains hints as to where one might turn to fill it in. For example, Psalm 90 could supply further help here, since it relates the necessity of God's existence not only to the idea of eternity, but also to that of creation *ex nihilo*, and all in a context of praise and worship (not a set of connections in which numbers would obviously be at home, although they adumbrate a possibility worth bearing in mind when accounting for the quasi-devotional attitudes of mystically inclined mathematicians and philosophers to these perfect, timeless entities). And Malcolm also suggests that grasping the point or purpose of religious language-games turns upon having access to a distinct array of emotions (such as guilt greater than which can be conceived).

A less charitable reader might query both gap-filling strategies. The first is questionable on the grounds that a genuinely useful grammatical explanation of the distinctively religious sense of necessary existence cannot be supplied simply by citing a religious text in which some of these distinguishing grammatical connections are made without explaining how and why they are made: at the very least, much more work is required (although one might perhaps think of philosophers such as Phillips as providing just that). The second seems dubious because Malcolm invokes religious guilt as something required if one is to understand the point or purpose of employing a concept as opposed to understanding its logic or grammar, and thereby conjures up a picture of the human forms of life with religious concept as having two analytically distinct elements—a logical or grammatical shell or skeleton, and a body of human emotional responses. This is a curiously positivist vision of logical form married to emotional matter, as if experiential content alone could perform the necessary conjuring trick with these dry grammatical bones; and it plays right into the hands of those who suspect that Wittgensteinians who reject accounts of religious discourse as having the character of empirical discourse must be endorsing essentially expressivist or emotivist accounts of it instead. Above all, however, this dualist vision should seem deeply puzzling from a Wittgensteinian point of view: for if meaning is manifest in use, then how could one, even in principle, grasp the grammar of a concept without grasping the point or purpose of using it? It is as if Malcolm imagines that we might be said to have successfully clarified the grammar of a concept even if it continues to appear to us to be an utterly arbitrary and absurd construction; but if it does so appear to us, then how can we be said to have appreciated its use, its mode of employment, at all?

From my point of view, however, the critical assumption with which Malcolm (and indeed any more powerful or elaborate position generated by supplementing Malcolm with Phillips) is working, and that neither the charitable nor the uncharitable response to this approach puts in question, is the idea that there is in principle a way of making perfectly good grammatical sense of all religious uses of words. After all, the deeper underlying presupposition of Malcolm's general strategy of comparing religious and non-religious modes of discourse is precisely that religious modes of discourse are just as substantial, coherent, and intelligible as their non-religious counterparts—that religious ways of tying together perfection, non-dependence, and necessary existence are fundamentally continuous with our ways of talking about the imperfections, dependencies, and contingencies of empirical objects, and that the nature and function of proofs in religious language-games resemble their nature and function in mathematical language-games. In short, then, Malcolm takes it to be empirically obvious that religious language-games are played, hence that they are possessed of a coherent grammar that can be intelligibly characterized, and so that our forms of life with religious language (just like our forms of life with any other kinds of language) simply must be accepted.

This assumption matters because it entails that neither of the two ways of inheriting the later Wittgenstein that dominate the current philosophical scene will find it possible to accept 'Grammatical Thomism' as a genuinely Wittgensteinian way of understanding the writings and method of Aquinas. More precisely, the willingness of the Grammatical Thomists to make an acknowledgement of the nonsensicality of religious discourse the beginning and end of their theology will immediately disqualify them as legitimate inheritors of Wittgenstein from the perspective of both traditions. For according to the first way of inheriting Wittgenstein (exemplified by Kenny and Rundle), the Grammatical Thomists are right in their perception of the nonsensicality of discourse about God, but fail to draw the appropriate Wittgensteinian conclusion from this—namely, that all such discourse thereby disqualifies itself from legitimate human use. Whereas according to the second (exemplified by Malcolm and Phillips), they are simply wrong to characterize religious discourse as nonsensical because it does have legitimate human uses (because, one might say, perfectly coherent if extremely distinctive religious language-games are played), and so the Grammatical Thomists must simply have failed to identify the particular grammar of those kinds of uses of words. In short: if religious discourse has a grammar, it cannot be nonsensical; and if it is nonsensical, then a grammar is precisely what it lacks. Either way, to call this theological project 'Grammatical Thomism' would be to fail to grasp the grammar of (Wittgensteinian) 'grammar'. And representatives of both ways of inheriting the later Wittgenstein might further unite in suspecting that Grammatical Thomists could only think of their positive or uncritical conception of nonsense as Wittgensteinian because they have illegitimately conflated the later Wittgenstein with his earlier Tractarian incarnation, and thereby given themselves permission to draw upon his early conception of mystical or ethico-religious propositions as necessarily hopeless attempts to articulate the inarticulable reality of the realm of transcendent value.

For two such different—indeed, mutually hostile—ways of inheriting Wittgenstein for the philosophy of religion to agree on the illegitimacy of the Grammatical Thomists' claimed allegiance to their patriarch may not be exactly startling (most viable ways of interpreting Wittgenstein will easily locate common non- or anti-Wittgensteinian enemies); but it might nevertheless prompt us to note that their very different ways of evaluating religious uses of language are predicated on a deeper agreement about a logically prior evaluative matter. For both those Wittgensteinians who regard religion as nonsensical and those who regard it as entirely coherent nevertheless agree that in Wittgensteinian hands or mouths 'nonsense' is necessarily a term of criticism; after all, it is precisely because it is a criticism that Wittgensteinians of Malcolm's or Phillips' stripe are committed to denying that it applies to religious utterances.

In Lecture Two, I want to interrogate the legitimacy of this deeper point of agreement. I want to suggest that the later Wittgenstein might plausibly be seen as countenancing a kind of nonsense that plays a deeply significant role in our life with language and so in our lives, and that guidance in understanding how this might be so can in fact be drawn from the role assigned to nonsense in his early work; but appreciating that guidance depends upon realizing that the early role of nonsense is not what most commentators take it to be. I will argue, with the help of Cora Diamond and the Brothers Grimm, that Wittgenstein's view of ethico-religious utterances (early and late) is that they are sheerly nonsensical (as opposed to being instances of illuminating nonsense, inevitably misfiring attempts to articulate what is ineffably so), and that that is precisely why we have a use for them. In other words, I propose to outline a way of understanding Wittgenstein's vision of the limits of sense that is significantly different from the standard reading of his early work, and from either of the standard ways of inheriting his later work. And in so doing, I hope to make it clear that the two traditions of interpreting Wittgenstein that have dominated our reception of him in the philosophy of religion and theology do not exhaust the available options—whether with respect to understanding the later Wittgenstein, or to understanding the possible and actual ways in which theology, religion, and nonsensicality might be related.

Once this exegetical ground is prepared, I will then be in a position—in Lecture Three—to show that, and how, Grammatical Thomism can be seen not only as an authentically Wittgensteinian enterprise, but also as a genuinely fruitful approach to theology and the philosophy of religion; here, the exemplary writings of Herbert McCabe will be clarified by juxtaposing them with the work of Denys Turner. But one of the most striking aspects of the Grammatical Thomist project from the point of view of a philosopher is that—especially in the hands of David Burrell—its vision of theology is tightly interwoven with its vision of language and of philosophy; so in Lectures Four and Five, I will examine and critically evaluate those further aspects of the project. In Lecture Four, my concern will be to connect the Grammatical Thomists' characteristic discounting or demystification of Aquinas' so-called theory of analogical uses of language with the later Wittgenstein's vision of language as—in terms provided by Stanley Cavell—inherently projective; and in Lecture Five, I will focus on the unappreciated extent to which the later Wittgenstein's *Philosophical Investigations* acknowledges the Grammatical Thomist conception of the internal relation between the pivotal role of perfections and transcendentals in theology and in philosophy. Finally, in Lecture Six, I will (with the help of Rai Gaita, Helmut Gollwitzer, and Abraham) confront the fundamental question that these analogies and comparisons—if found to be plausible—inevitably throw up: how are we to understand the relation between theology and philosophy in the human form of life?

Lecture Two

The Flounder and the Fisherman's Wife

Tractarian Ethics, the Mystical, and the Religious

In Lecture One, I identified the two main ways in which Wittgenstein's later philosophical methods had been inherited and applied to the field of the philosophy of religion, and suggested that since both (whilst differing in many other ways) agreed that identifying a stretch of discourse as nonsensical amounted to a definitive critique of (let's say) its human significance, then both would be bound to regard Grammatical Thomism as essentially alien to the Wittgensteinian philosophical spirit, insofar as it appears to make a theological virtue of the fact that religious language directed towards the transcendent Christian God necessarily outstrips the limits of sense. In this lecture, I want to make a case for reading Wittgenstein's attitude towards nonsense differently, in both his early and his later work: and since making that case with respect to his later work becomes less difficult once it is made with respect to his early work, I propose to begin with the *Tractatus Logico-Philosophicus*. In so doing, I will be making extensive use of the work of Cora Diamond, whose way of interpreting the early Wittgenstein's views on the non-sensicality of ethico-religious discourse grows out of her more general commitment to what has been called an 'austere' reading of the role of nonsense in the *Tractatus*, and so a 'resolute' reading of the philosophical method employed in that book. It is this method which engenders its notorious concluding declaration that anyone who understands its author must recognize that the elucidatory propositions that make it up (propositions that appear to express a variety of substantial views about the essence of language, thought, and world, and that must presumably provide whatever grounds there are for this conclusion itself) are nonsensical.[1]

The traditional way of understanding that declaration is to invoke what has been called a substantial conception of nonsense. According to this approach, the metaphysical propositions of the *Tractatus* exemplify a kind of nonsense that is distinct from mere gibberish: it is that which results from violations of logical syntax, from the combination of individually intelligible ingredients in an illegitimate way. By deliberately constructing such nonsensical propositions, the author of the *Tractatus* means to direct our attention to metaphysical insights which cannot be expressed in genuine propositions, but which genuine propositions nevertheless show by virtue of their intelligibility—that is, by virtue of one or another aspect of their logical form, which they share with the reality that they are consequently capable of depicting either truly or falsely. This shared logical form, with all its metaphysical implications, might therefore be revealed by the necessarily hopeless attempt to speak in a manner which refuses to respect it in some specific way—by the, as it were, determinate unintelligibility of such violations of logical syntax. This is why Wittgenstein thinks that speaking nonsense might nevertheless be philosophically illuminating, and hence believes that coming to recognize that certain propositions are instances of (substantial) nonsense is a criterion of philosophical insight into necessarily ineffable metaphysical truths.

According to a resolute reading of the *Tractatus*, by contrast, for a string of signs to be nonsensical is always and only for at least one of those signs, in that context, to lack a meaning. To use an example Wittgenstein offers in section 5.4733, 'Socrates is identical' is nonsense not because a name and the sign for identity have been illegitimately combined, but rather because the sign 'identical' has not been assigned a (presumably adjectival) meaning for this context (even though, in another context, it can and does function as a sign of identity); and all

---

[1] The following, necessarily brief, general, and highly selective account of what I will be calling 'resolute' (as opposed to 'substantial') readings of the *Tractatus* is particularly indebted to two long and recent essays exemplifying that approach: James Conant's 'The Method of the *Tractatus*', in E. Reck (ed.), *From Frege to Wittgenstein* (Oxford: OUP, 2002); and James Conant and Cora Diamond, 'On Reading the *Tractatus* Resolutely', in M. Kölbel and B. Weiss (eds), *Wittgenstein's Lasting Significance* (London: Routledge, 2004).

of the nonsensical propositions of the *Tractatus* which the substantial reading regards as conveying ineffable metaphysical insight are nonsensical in exactly the same way as is 'Socrates is identical'—logically speaking, they too simply contain at least one sign to which no meaning has been assigned in and for that context.

Hence, according to the resolute reading, when Wittgenstein suggests that identifying his own propositions as nonsense is a criterion for coming to understand him, he means coming to recognize that even what seems to be substantial nonsense is in fact no more than mere gibberish (logically speaking). He is not trying to identify ineffable truths that he means to convey to us by violating the rules of logical syntax; he is rather attempting to wean us away from the illusion that there are any ineffable truths—and in particular from the final, most tenacious version of that illusion, according to which, even after recognizing that genuinely ineffable truths must lie beyond the limits of language and thought, we continue to think that they might be hinted at or gestured towards, and so that we might see beyond those limits, by the deliberate construction of self-destructing pieces of substantial nonsense. He does so by first appearing to share our conviction that there are such ineffable truths, then inviting us to discover and reflect upon the emptiness of these putative thoughts in all their versions, and then—finally—encouraging us to let go of the very idea that philosophy might be possessed of any such subject matter.

One might, then, say that the fundamental point of the *Tractatus* on this reading is that of identifying and aiming to overcome our attraction to the idea that there is something we cannot do in philosophy. The notion of substantial nonsense is that of pseudo-propositions that are unintelligible, but determinately so; they therefore seem to specify a thought that we cannot think—an identifiable place in the region that lies beyond the limits of sense, something specific that exceeds our mental grasp. But of course, if the limits of sense are the limits of intelligibility, then nothing whatever lies beyond them; they are not boundaries fencing us off from a further determinate or determinable region, and so not limitations upon our capacity to think or speak. To recognize that the only species of nonsense is gibberish is, accordingly, to recognize that the limits of sense are not limitations, and so to acknowledge that there is nothing (no specifiable thing, no conceivable task or activity of speech or thought) that we cannot do.

2.1 Fairy-Tale Ethics

Adjudicating the relative merits of the traditional and resolute ways of reading the *Tractatus* is obviously a significant and complex matter; but it is equally obvious that I can't prosecute that task here. What concerns me in the current context is rather the manner in which adopting a resolute reading of the early philosophy opens up a different way of interpreting its notorious characterization of ethico-religious utterances as nonsensical. Since many of these Tractarian ideas reappear more accessibly in the context of a short lecture on ethics that Wittgenstein delivered in 1929, I want—following Diamond—to use that lecture as a way into the obscurities of the earlier text.[2]

Wittgenstein's lecture distinguishes between a relative and an absolute sense in which evaluative terms are used. If I say that this lectern is good, I mean that it serves its specific purposes well, and so I judge its merits by reference to a predetermined purpose; similarly, if I say that this is the right road for you, I mean that it brings you most directly to Cambridge, and so I judge its merits relative to a prior goal that I believe you have. The relativity of these judgements has two implications. First, if you reject the goal or purpose relative to which I make the judgement, you can perfectly intelligibly reject the judgement—if you didn't want to get to Cambridge today, then that wasn't the right road for you; and second, I can always recast such evaluative judgements so as to bring out their implicit invocation of, and so their internal relation to, matters of fact— 'this is the right road if you happen to have a certain desire (namely, to get to Cambridge in the shortest time)'. Judgements of absolute value are, Wittgenstein claims, very different: their absoluteness resides in the fact that they make no reference to a goal or purpose that you might intelligibly reject, and are not grounded in some matter of fact (say, about your desires or motives) that might be otherwise (and so might permit you to avoid its demands).

This distinction is intuitively plausible. Imagine someone who tells a lie, is criticized for acting badly, and tries to defend himself by saying that he has no desire to behave well: would we say 'Fair enough—sorry for the misunderstanding' or would we say 'You ought to behave well

---

[2] 'Lecture on Ethics', in J.C. Klagge and A. Nordmann (eds), *Wittgenstein: Philosophical Occasions* (Indianapolis: Hackett, 1993), hereafter 'LE'.

whether you want to or not.' But Wittgenstein recognizes that the latter reaction is more puzzling than it may at first appear. For if we attempt to understand judgements of absolute value on the model of judgements of relative value, then we would have to say that a road that was not just right but absolutely right would have to be one that everyone with utter necessity would have to go along, or feel ashamed for not doing so; and a state of affairs that was not just good but absolutely good would be one that everyone—regardless of their tastes or inclinations—would necessarily bring about or feel ashamed for not doing so. In short: if what is essential to relative value judgements (their conditionality) is necessarily absent in absolute value judgements, then we cannot coherently regard them as two species of the same genus. But if that is not the right way of understanding judgements of absolute value, then what is?

Wittgenstein's view in the lecture appears to be that the distinguishing mark of judgements of absolute value is precisely their failure to make sense: the verbal expressions of experiences of absolute value are essentially nonsensical. One of his examples is someone who claims to feel absolutely safe. We are familiar with the idea of feeling safe from a wide range of specific dangers—a rabid dog, a threat to our reputation, a tsunami; but in all these cases what it means to be safe is determined by the specific nature of the threat, and we can always envisage what it would be like if we were not safe from the relevant threat—that is, envisage what our current safety in fact depends upon, and how those conditions might be otherwise. But to feel absolutely safe is to invoke an idea of safety that is essentially unconditional—a sense of being safe that is not a matter of being safe from anything in particular, hence is not keyed to any particular threat, and so is not vulnerable to any change of contingent circumstances or conditions, a safety that could not conceivably be overcome or subverted. In effect, a familiar, intelligible use of words has here been recast in such a way as to resist our familiar ways of making sense of it; and on Wittgenstein's view it is only such recastings of evaluative words that are capable of registering the kinds of experience and judgement that he wants to call matters of absolute value. 'I see not only that no description that I can think of would do to describe what I mean by absolute value, but that I would reject every significant description that anyone could possibly suggest, *ab initio*, on the grounds of its significance' (LE, 44).

On the traditional reading of the early Wittgenstein, his post-Tractarian position here would be one according to which judgements of absolute value do have a real object or referent, but one that is supernatural rather than natural—one lying beyond or outside the world; and it is because of their essential reference to a realm that transcends the natural (more broadly the domain of the factual, or that of possible human experience) that they fail to make sense. In other words, there are absolute evaluative truths, but we are incapable of giving expression to them: we can only gesture towards them by repeatedly running up against the boundaries of language. According to a resolute reading, this idea of inexpressible evaluative truths would have to be discarded as devoid of sense, and along with it the whole thrust of the traditional interpretation of Wittgenstein's early stance towards value; but what of the judgements of absolute value of which that traditional idea was supposed to make sense? Any resolute reader would have to regard them too as devoid of sense—as simply and sheerly nonsensical; but according to Diamond, this is entirely consistent with seeing their employment as intelligibly motivated, and so as possessed of significance—a significance they can and do possess (not despite but) by virtue of their nonsensicality. For it is open to a resolute reader to understand the use of such expressions as indicating a refusal on their users' part to accept certain apparently unavoidable ways of assigning sense to them.

Consider the *Tractatus* invocation of the happy man (as opposed to the unhappy man), presented as the bearer of a will that is not only good but transcendentally good, and characterizable as one whose happiness is utterly unaffected by the way things go in the world. We might well feel inclined to say that such a man incarnates an attitude of satisfaction with the world as a whole. Someone might then point out to us that talk of an 'attitude of satisfaction with the world as a whole' is modelled on talk of attitudes to something in particular, some way that things are within the world that might satisfy or dissatisfy us; but no sense is thereby assigned to an attitude of dissatisfaction to the world as such, however things may be within it—so that last phrase only appears to make sense. This intervention might very well lead us to preface any future utterance of this ethical sentence with words like 'I am inclined to say . . .'; but if Diamond's Wittgenstein is right we would not necessarily lose our inclination to say it. Such framing would mark a certain gain in self-awareness, a liberation from un-self-consciously taking nonsense for sense; but continuing to use the sentences so framed would mark our continuing to feel that just these sentences (modelled on meaningful ones but unmoored from their patterns of use) express the sense we want to make—or rather, that our intentions in uttering them were essentially incompatible with making sense.

On this view, to describe the intention of the would-be engager in ethics as necessarily frustrated by the use of any intelligible sentence is simply to say that she refuses to accept any intelligible candidate articulation of her intention as an articulation *of that intention*. No assignment of meaning to her utterance will satisfy her—not because she wants to assign it an ineffable meaning, but because she finds satisfaction precisely in refusing to find any available assignments of meaning satisfying. After all, as we saw earlier in this lecture, a resolute reader's understanding of the use of nonsensical metaphysical propositions by the author of the *Tractatus* depends upon distinguishing the (un-)intelligibility of his propositions from the intelligibility of his motive in employing them, and more specifically upon identifying a therapeutic motive for which only nonsensical propositions will serve. Diamond is in effect proposing that we exploit exactly the same distinction in understanding that author's (or indeed anyone's) use of expressions of absolute value. Understanding the user of such forms of words then becomes a matter of understanding why someone might find assignments of significance to such propositions essentially unsatisfying.

In both the *Tractatus* and the later lecture, the specific kind of meaning-assignment to ethical utterances that is being resisted is that characteristic of fact-stating, empirical discourse in general, and of empirical psychological discourse in particular. Hence, the absolute or unconditional nature of the refusal indicates a sense of absolute discontinuity between the ethical and the empirical world. As Diamond puts it:

That which I take myself to see in myself or another if I think of that person as having a [good or] evil will—that thought of mine about a person—has no room in the sphere of thoughts about the world of empirical facts. Put there it is not about what I wanted it to be about. (EIM,[3] 85–6)

---

[3] 'Ethics, Imagination and the Method of the *Tractatus*', in A. Crary and R. Read (eds), *The New Wittgenstein* (London: Routledge, 2000), hereafter 'EIM'.

Such a refusal is not an objection to the very idea of evaluative uses of language that are logically or conceptually tied to the natural realm, and so capable of being rendered intelligible by those means. Evaluating lecterns or roads can be understood perfectly well in naturalistic terms; so can the use of language to alter people's feelings and attitudes, or to express adherence to prescriptive principles, or to guide action; these are the judgements of relative value to which the lecture on ethics refers. But for just that reason, such uses fail to capture what Wittgenstein means by 'absolute value' or 'the ethical as the mystical'; that meaning is precisely given expression by his refusal of any such ways of assigning evaluative sense to his ethical sentences (and so would be obliterated by any philosophical account—whether Wittgensteinian or not—that took it for granted that any meaningful ethical sentences must fit within such fact-related or -conditioned modes of language use). The point of his refusal is thus to draw a sharp contrast between two *kinds* of evil (and hence two kinds of good): 'evil [that] is ... inconsequential ..., something close to home ... something [not] very bad to which one might become accustomed, and [evil as] something terrible, black, and wholly alien that you cannot even get near'.

To see what this distinction might involve, Diamond recalls the ethical vision of some of the most famous fairy tales compiled by the brothers Grimm. Take Rumpelstiltskin: the boastful miller and the greedy king who manipulate the miller's daughter and set her the impossible task for which she requires Rumpelstiltskin's help are not at all nice decent folk; but the tale does not connect their badness with our capacity to respond to evil as unapproachable and terrible, the kind of evil incarnated in Rumpelstiltskin (an evil exactly as other-worldly as the transformative powers he hires out to the new queen). For Rumpelstiltskin not only wants to abduct someone else's child, but—as we discover when the queen's servant overhears his gleeful, dancing fireside song connecting the child's arrival with cooking—to devour it. Little wonder the tale assigns a very different fate to the miller and the king than it does to Rumpelstiltskin, who tears himself in two with self-consuming rage. Sensible, well-meaning commentators—articulating responses that we too might initially have to this tale—argue that Rumpelstiltskin is as much a helper as a villain in comparison with the girl's father and husband, even that he is the traumatized victim of loneliness; but in so doing, they reduce his immorality to an everyday mediocre kind, essentially explicable in terms of familiar psychological syndromes. This is bringing Rumpelstiltskin's evil into the domain of the empirical world with a vengeance; and it thereby evades the very ethical contrast that the tale is designed to register.

Or recall the tale of the fisherman who rescues a magic flounder, who offers in gratitude to grant his rescuer whatever he wishes; the fisherman's wife begins her exploitation of this opportunity by asking for a better home and ends by expressing dissatisfaction at the sun's and the moon's rising independently of her will—at which point a cosmically destructive storm arises from the flounder's ocean and returns her to the pigsty in which they had originally been living. Being dissatisfied at having to live in a pigsty is not only not evil, it may even seem essential to anyone's sense of self-respect; so the wife's transition to her climactic dissatisfaction may accordingly appear to be a seamlessly comprehensible (even if ethically degrading) transformation. But to find her final demand an intelligible endpoint of some comprehensible worldly process of moral deterioration, one must fail to see that wanting the world to conform to her will amounts to wanting it not to be a world at all; to put it otherwise, one must find intelligible the idea of her occupying God's perspective on the world. To see nothing more in such dissatisfactions than an unwise but understandable overextension of an essentially healthy self-regard would be to obliterate the distinction between genuine human needs and world-extinguishing hubris. Refusing to draw such distinctions may appear as realism, expressive of down-to-earth rational disdain for mystery and mysticism; but in truth it simply obliterates their distinctive ethical significance.

My claim, following Diamond, is that the early Wittgenstein's removal of thought and talk about the good and evil will from the empirical realm as such is essentially another way of marking that contrast—one of a number of possible techniques of language through which it might be indicated and maintained. The dissatisfaction of the fisherman's wife is, I would suggest, akin to that of Wittgenstein's unhappy man, who is dissatisfied at the world regardless of how things go within it, hence not so much dissatisfied with *how* that world is as with the bare fact of its existence, with its sheer independent reality—its refusal to meet the conditions he lays down, to submit to his control. And it is vital to see that both literary techniques for marking this discontinuity simultaneously acknowledge an underlying continuity, and thereby emphasize that the nature of the distinction resists our attempts to comprehend it.

According to the brothers Grimm, the cosmic dissatisfaction of the fisherman's wife is intuitable even in her initial desire to have a cosy little house rather than a pigsty: the tale explicitly marks this by noting that the sea is already faintly discoloured and mildly turbulent when the fisherman brings his wife's first wish to the flounder's attention, quite as if the world-annihilating storm she eventually unleashes is already gathering its energies. So it is internal to the brothers' way of thinking that the wife's catastrophic hubris is at once something absolutely out of the ordinary, and yet always already lurking beneath the surface of the most innocuous expressions of human will. Her terrible evil is essentially irreducible to the terms of everyday moral and psychological under-standing, and yet somehow shadows or haunts both them and the terrain that is their *Heimat*: that is why, however much violence we must do to their familiar modes of use, it is precisely these words (the ones we employ to talk intelligibly about intra-worldly objects of desire and dissatisfaction) to which the violence must be done if what we intend by our utterance is to be satisfactorily articulated. Nothing other than the failure of sense resulting from that violence could convey the simultan-eous continuity and discontinuity we mean to capture; one might say that it is the unintelligibility of *these* forms of words that alone can articulate the resistance of such evil to our comprehension.

It may seem that this kind of resolute reading of expressions of absolute value comes dangerously close to the model of 'substantial nonsense' that traditional readings use to understand the philosophical or metaphysical propositions that make up the *Tractatus*. After all, the nonsensicality here attributed to expressions of absolute value is a matter of their users deploying words that have a determinate significance in other contexts in a way that deliberately transgresses that mode of making sense of them. But the traditional reader thinks that Tractarian philosophical propositions are built out of subpropositional expressions that fully retain their familiar sense, whilst being combined in such a way as to cancel out sense at the level of the proposition; the model is that of individually intelligible propositional ingredients unintelligibly combined. By contrast, Diamond attributes no sense—familiar or otherwise—to the words that comprise expressions of absolute value: she suggests rather that we can make sense of their being so employed, and so of those employing them, if we can see their lack of sense in this evaluative context as a denial or deconstruction of the sense they make in other evaluative contexts—as a stripping away of those specific patterns of sense-making.

In so doing, Diamond brings to bear two Tractarian distinctions: that between understanding the meaning of an expression and understanding its user, and that between what pertains to logic and what falls outside it—matters of psychology, and empirical phenomena more broadly (including culture and history). Because the constituent terms of expressions of absolute value make specific kinds of sense elsewhere, their nonsensicality in this context (what from the point of view of logic is their merely material presence as signs lacking symbolic meaning) is, viewed psychologically, a matter of non-sensicality: we experience them not as simply lacking sense but as lacking *that* particular sense, as deprived of or refusing *that* familiar meaning (so that each bare mark is marked by the present absence of its symbolic individuality, by that which its user's refusal necessarily invokes). Appreciating this is not a matter of grasping the peculiar internal logic of an expression of absolute value (since it has none), but of grasping what Nietzsche might call its genealogy; we appreciate the peculiar significance of uttering such nonsense by seeing it as an intelligible outworking of the broader forms of human life within which the words uttered have uses whose internal logic and overall significance can be more straightforwardly grasped.

Of course, part of what is bewildering about such evaluative phenomena is that what we may see as incomprehensible is seen by others as utterly everyday—just as we can easily imagine readers of the Grimm tales who sense no cosmic evil in the initial responses of the fisherman's wife (and are correspondingly more likely to want to explain away or dismiss the Grimms' ways of connecting those initial responses to what Wittgenstein would call transcendental good and evil). Such phenomena will thereby tend to isolate individuals, disclosing others as opaque to them and themselves as opaque to those others; reality's resistance to our understanding reveals us as essentially resistant to one another's understanding—inasmuch as those to whom ethics involves transcendental good and evil will seem incomprehensible to those who find nothing within them (no impulses, intentions, or convictions) with which such deliberately nonsensical formulations might resonate.

And it is not as if those impulses, intentions, and convictions are entirely transparent to their possessors. On the contrary: those who recognize unapproachably terrible evil in the fisherman's wife can do so only because they are capable of imaginatively entering into the perspective of someone they conceive of as dissatisfied by the world's failure to submit to his will, which amounts to attempting to inhabit one kind of attachment to nonsense. When, as Diamond puts it, 'I enter imaginatively into the seeing of it as sense, I as it were become the person who thinks he thinks it. I treat that person's nonsense in imagination as if I took it to be an intelligible sentence of a language I understand, *something I find in myself the possibility of meaning*' (EIM, 81). So to intuit terrible evil in the fisherman's wife or Rumpelstiltskin depends upon finding in myself the kinds of impulses and intentions that find expression in the nonsense that articulates that kind of evil, and that I imagine another saying in her heart insofar as I do understand her. To identify incomprehensible evil in another thus depends upon a willingness to acknowledge a similarly incomprehensible possibility in myself.

What, then, of the transcendental good will? In order to intuit its presence in another, which presumably means being compelled to characterize that other in terms of a kind of piety in action, an ability to look with a clear eye at the world's vicissitudes and to acknowledge unconditionally its independence from his will, one necessarily resorts to nonsense phrases, and so registers a kind of resistance to the understanding in such goodness. But that resistance to sense also involves a perception of the miraculousness of such goodness, the sheer incomprehensibility of its realization in the world, the utter inexplicability of such radical self-abnegation in terms of our best naturalistic patterns of moral and psychological explanation. And if one can imaginatively enter into the perspective of such a good will in another, that will be because one is able to acknowledge similar impulses and intentions in oneself—because one is willing to relate to oneself as inexplicably but undeniably capable of goodness beyond virtue as well as evil beyond vice.

2.2 Anselm Revisited

These connections between ethics, reality's resistance to our understanding, and the mysteriousness of other people will recur, and receive a more expansive treatment, later in this set of lectures. For present purposes, however, what matters is that, when Diamond shifts the focus of her concern from the early to the later writings of Wittgenstein, she maintains her interest in the uses to which nonsense might be put; and in one of her most important essays, she focuses on a distinctively religious use for such nonsense. In 'Riddles and Anselm's Riddle',[4] Diamond contests Norman Malcolm's reading of Anselm's ontological argument by making a very different use of the comparison that (as we saw) is central to Malcolm's own reading—that between mathematics and religion. But whereas Malcolm focuses on the legitimacy of mathematical talk of necessary existence insofar as that is anchored by an established proof of a given theorem (such as there being an infinite number of primes), Diamond shifts our attention from theorems to conjectures, in order to exploit Wittgenstein's comparison of a mathematical conjecture that lacks a proof to a riddle for which we have not found a solution.[5]

Suppose I ask: 'What has four legs in the morning, two at noon, and three in the evening?' To solve this riddle, you need to know more than what that form of words describes; you need to know *how* it describes it—to see how a human being might be seen as fitting that description, how those words might be seen as a description of human existence. If so, then until we have the solution to the riddle, together with an understanding of how it counts as a solution to it, to that extent we lack an understanding of the riddle phrase that the question employs, and so lack an understanding of the question.

And yet we can seek the solution to such riddles. How? We might think that this is because we can at least judge that any solution will have to meet certain conditions. It seems clear in advance, for example, that if something has four legs, it must have more than two legs; but that would imply that, whatever the solution to our riddle might turn out to be, it can't be a human being. This shows that we no more understand the further conditions we might impose on a solution to our riddle than we understand the riddle itself: part of grasping its solution *as a solution* will be grasping how it can be said to meet these ancillary conditions, and so those conditions can't be said to control what will count as a solution. But it also shows that our imaginative engagement with the riddle is controlled by *something*—by existing patterns of use in our language, on the basis of which the riddle phrase has been constructed.

---

[4] In *The Realistic Spirit* (Cambridge: MIT Press, 1991).
[5] Cf. Wittgenstein, *Lectures on the Foundations of Mathematics, Cambridge 1939*, ed. C. Diamond (Chicago: University of Chicago Press, 1989), p. 84.

In the case of this riddle, there are existing patterns of employing number words, of describing animal anatomy and its supplements, and of measuring time; and familiar ways of extending those patterns—for example, comparing different ways of measuring time (measuring the course of a life in terms of the progress of a day). Finding a solution to the Sphinx's riddle is a matter of finding a way to see something as inviting us to project all those patterns on to it in an appropriate way; but what we need in order to answer it is not something of which we have been given a determinate description, but something that it will strike us as right to call by the riddle phrase. The familiarity of the phrase's construction, and of its grammatical connections with other phrases, is what orients our seeking, and gives the phrase whatever meaning we wish to say that it has at this pre-solution stage, but without allowing us simply to read off what we will be prepared to count as its solution, or indeed whether there is one.

Wittgenstein sees an analogy here with our relation to a mathematical conjecture that lacks a proof. By fixing its place in the system of mathematical propositions, a proof gives the conjecture a determinate meaning it hitherto lacked, although the task of seeking a proof of it is given such orientation as it has, and so the conjecture has whatever meaning we may wish to say that it has for us prior to the construction of that proof, by virtue of our familiarity with other mathematical concepts and procedures on analogy with which the conjecture has been constructed. But we may conclude that nothing will count as an application of the relevant phrase, for example 'the rational number p/q which when squared gives 2'. This phrase puts together meaningful mathematical concepts on analogy with meaningful mathematical propositions; but if by following out these and other analogies we can show that any such p cannot be odd, and cannot be even either, then we may abandon the idea that the original phrase is meaningful, because the only alternative would be to have a system in which we would call something a cardinal number even though it was neither odd nor even. A *reductio* proof of this kind can do its work without assuming that the phrase to which it relates makes sense; we play at using a phrase of that shape as an assumption, and establish further conditions on that to which it may be held to apply, and then conclude that we are not willing to accept that anything could meet all those conditions—at which point we stop playing with the possibility that the phrase makes any mathematical sense. We conclude, in other words, that the promise of a necessary connection articulated by the 'conditions' we 'established' is unfulfilled.

Diamond suggests that Anselm's ontological argument can be illuminatingly regarded as a working out of just such promissory connections. The riddle phrase 'that than which nothing greater can be conceived' (hereafter TTWNGCBC) is itself constructed on the basis of a familiar model (great, greater, greatest, greatest conceivable); and Anselm draws upon existing linguistic connections between lacking something, being limited, being dependent, coming into existence and having a beginning in order to establish that if we were to call anything TTWNGCBC, then it would be something that had no beginning. The point is not that (as Malcolm would have it) on the basis of our understanding of TTWNGCBC, we know that it has no beginning, as if we were simply reminding ourselves of a language-game we know how to play; we are rather forging the outer shell of a necessary connection in a language we do not yet know how to speak. In contemplating TTWNGCBC, we are entertaining familiar words combined in a familiar pattern, and we don't rule out the possibility of a new language-game in which that word-shape has a place and in which we might find ourselves at home; but if that possibility were realized, it would be the discovery *of* a logical space, not a discovery within such an established space.

Anselm's emphasis on the difference between existence in the understanding and existence in reality can then be seen as a (potentially misleading) way of distinguishing between ideas that we can, and those that we cannot, conceive of being the result of human inventive capacities. He wants to emphasize that our conception of what is possible might itself be shown up by reality—that reality might show us not only that something is the case that we imagined was not, but that something beyond what we had ever taken to be possible, something beyond anything we could imagine as possible, was actual. If so, then TTWNGCBC could not be anything we can imagine human beings imagining; for we can think of something greater than that—namely something that could not conceivably have been conceived by us, something in the light of which the products of our religious imagination appear as a queer collection of bloodless abstractions or sentimental projections, something that reveals a logical space where none had seemed to exist.

Now, if anything we were willing to count as TTWNGCBC must be something that we cannot imagine having merely imagined, it must also be such that we could not imagine it never having existed. For if we could, then we could separate the idea of it from its actuality, could make sense of the possibility of making sense of it *as* a mere possibility to which nothing actual happened to correspond; and then we could conceive of something greater than it—namely, something whose actuality is a condition for the possibility of conceiving it, something without which it is inconceivable that we could possess a language of any kind for it. Hence, anything we were willing to count as TTWNGCBC would have to be something whose non-existence could not be conceived, something whose conceivability is itself conceivable only on condition of its actuality.

In the case of ordinary riddles, and mathematical proofs, Diamond argues that it is only when we discover that there is a solution to the riddle, and how it counts as a solution, that we fully understand the question the riddle poses; before this, the relevant phrases or propositions have only promissory meaning. But in the case of TTWNGCBC, Anselm has established that every statement we can make about it has, and can only have, a promissory meaning; the full transparency of that language to us is ruled out, because if it were to have a meaning we could fully grasp now, then we could conceive of something greater than whatever those words describe (namely, something whose nature exceeds the grasp of any concepts of which we can even conceive). And of course that form of words ('something whose nature exceeds the grasp of any concept of which we can even conceive') is no more fully transparent to us than any other form of words to which it is 'grammatically' linked, via the outer shell of a 'necessary connection'. All are 'allusions' to a 'language' we cannot even conceive of speaking before actually finding ourselves in a position to speak it—a language given to us by the being to whom it applies, and whose revelation of himself will effect the radical conversion of all our existing concepts of him.

Accordingly, in the sense in which Wittgenstein normally claims that words have a grammar—the sense in which Malcolm assumes that all religious discourse has a grammar—these words do not; they are grammatically distinctive in that that they have no grammar, but only a 'grammar'. On Diamond's view, that is what a close attention to the way we employ such words will reveal. She is not denying that we do talk of God in the context of honest, transparent language-games, whose grammar tells us what kind of thing is being spoken of, and which

might well be illuminated by the approach of Wittgensteinian philosophers of religion such as Malcolm and Phillips; but she *is* claiming that
whatever we are talking about in such games is not a possible solution to
the riddle posed by the phrase TTWNGCBC—for that is a form of words
which does not tell us the kind of thing to which it refers, but rather
stands in need of a determination of meaning, one which must come not
from us but from whatever it turns out to apply to. Since ordinary riddle
phrases can be given meaning by us, insofar as we can find a way of
meaning them, Diamond talks of riddle phrases such as TTWNGCBC as
embodying a great riddle (alluding thereby to Wittgenstein's Tractarian
invocation of the 'question' of the meaning of life, which he tells us will
remain even were we to arrive at answers to all our articulable, grammatically coherent questions, and to which he tells us there is no
conceivable solution, only a dissolution of the question).

Hence, those who claim that there is a solution to the great riddle
cannot mean that they grasp *how* that solution is a solution to the riddle
(since they would then be able to translate the riddle phrase into, or at
least relate it intelligibly to, an honest bit of language, something ruled
out by the phrase itself). They can only mean that they know *that*
something is the solution, without knowing how—rather as if I were to
take someone's word that they have a proof of a mathematical proposition, even if I don't know what it is. This, Diamond claims, is Anselm's
position with respect to the fool of the Psalm: Anselm thinks that the fool
cannot rule out TTWNGCBC as a word-shape which might be given a
use, whereas for Anselm itself it is already the shape of a truth he has
been given. If the fool were to rule it out, he would be purporting to judge
something that leaves him without the linguistic footing for any judgement of his own about it. By the same token, however, the only demonstration that such-and-such *is* TTWNGCBC is one that cannot be
separated from the apparent authority of the being in question (for
example, the resurrected Jesus, who shows what would otherwise have
remained invisible—that the Messianic passages of the Old Testament
refer to him). In other words, even the bare identification of something as
TTWNGCBC is a truth of faith, or it is nothing.

This leaves us with the following dialectical situation. If the fool were
to deny any identification of such-and-such as TTWNGCBC, then to
Anselm he is like someone who, groping for a solution to the Sphinx's
riddle, thinks 'it certainly can't be a man'. The fool simply doesn't

understand his own words, and his atheistic belief depends upon that failure of understanding. From the fool's own point of view, however, TTWNGCBC is either at home in a language-game, or it remains a (non-great) riddle devoid of any solution (since none in his view has been authoritatively identified, let alone shown be to a solution), or it is a mere form of words; and no argument on Anselm's part can show any of these responses to be incoherent. What one sees as incomprehensible but undeniable, the other sees as undeniably empty; hence each resists the other's understanding.

Diamond's conclusion may sound remarkably like Malcolm's distinction between proofs and faith; but she reaches it by rejecting every step of his reading of both Anselm and Wittgenstein, and three of those rejections are particularly pertinent here. First, she emphasizes that Wittgenstein's work allows that a form of words which has a place in some activity might nevertheless be expressive of deep confusion; hence we cannot show that people who wish to think of the God of the Old Testament as a genocidal maniac are conceptually or philosophically confused simply because language-games are played in which such things cannot be said of God (because he is conceived of as perfect). Indeed, Anselm might well countenance the possibility of our coming to say of that game, and of religious forms of life as a whole, that they are 'judged and condemned by TTWNGCBC'.

Second, where Malcolm sees a coherent expression with a grammar, Diamond sees a particular kind of riddle phrase—not only words seeking a sense, and so a grammar, but words for which sense can only come from without. From Diamond's perspective, one could charitably say that this is why Malcolm is tempted to distinguish the logical coherence of Anselm's concept of God from its point or purpose, whilst simultaneously and incoherently trying to suggest that the gap is bridged by the emotional content of a form of life; his hollowed-out notion of grammar as mere logical form dimly registers the fact that it is internal to the significance of these words that they have only a 'grammar'.

Third, whereas Malcolm is inclined to assume that the thinking and seeking expressed in such terminology as TTWNGCBC belongs exclusively to those who play religious language-games, and hence participate in religious forms of life, Diamond thinks that such language has a life of its own—that it belongs to anyone; the *Heimat* of such questions is our life with language, not any particular language-game. For the tendency to ask them does not depend on any form of life more specific than that of speaking; it is as much something primitive or given as our responses to other people—no more and no less than natural to us speakers (which of course means that for some people it does not come naturally at all). Such questions arise from our ability and willingness to play with linguistic analogies, to find certain ways of extending our ways with words to be natural and worth pursuing, to catch our imaginations in such a way as to hold open the possibility of a possibility of sense before we have established any technique of use corresponding to it.

For Diamond, then, if our philosophical recountings sever the grammatical uses of religious concepts within religious language-games from their 'grammatical', riddling or sense-resistant uses, we simultaneously occlude a vital dimension of their religious significance, and a vital point of contact or continuity between those for whom religious forms of life are natural and their non-religious human fellows. And this vision of religion's place in human forms of life follows from her willingness to put imagination and inclination rather than rule-governed techniques at the heart of Wittgenstein's vision of language. For our love of riddles exemplifies the interplay of what comes naturally with our capacity for imaginative play; our ways of responding to mathematical conjectures manifest its centrality to the *Heimat* of reason; and Anselm's way with TTWNGCBC shows how, at its fullest extent, that interplay can acknowledge its own limits—by acknowledging the possibility that reality might utterly overturn our best efforts to imagine what might lie beyond our wildest imaginings.

Having laid out the basic elements of this alternative way of reading Wittgenstein's view of nonsense or the limits of sense, I can at last return in Lecture Three to a more detailed consideration of the Grammatical Thomist project, and show in equal detail how that project's emphasis on the nonsensicality of theological utterances not only renders it compatible with a basically Wittgensteinian orientation to language, but also allows us to find deeper ranges of significance in Wittgenstein's later way of philosophizing than would otherwise be apparent.

Lecture Three

Grammatical Thomism
Five Ways of Refusing to Make Sense

In Lecture One, I laid out two dominant ways of inheriting Wittgenstein's later philosophy according to which the idea of 'Grammatical Thomism'—by virtue of its willingness to embrace the nonsensicality of language directed towards knowing and naming God—must appear to be a contradiction in terms. In Lecture Two, I used the work of Cora Diamond to show that there is another way of reading Wittgenstein, both early and late, such that his identification of a sentence or stretch of discourse as nonsensical need not be taken to preclude a willingness to find in it a specific and intelligible pattern of use, and thereby to acknowledge its potential human significance. In this lecture, I want to suggest that Diamond's reading of Anselm's ontological argument in the light of riddling uses of language can help us to see that the Grammatical Thomist project, and specifically the Aquinas they read into or out of the opening pages of the *Summa*, can genuinely claim to be inheriting Wittgenstein's later way of doing philosophy.

3.1 Wittgensteinian Worries about Grammatical Thomism

Before making that case for what one might call the 'grammaticality' of Grammatical Thomism, however, the Wittgensteinian case against is sufficiently powerful to be worth outlining and evaluating. Its lineaments can most easily be seen if we focus on a canonical Grammatical Thomist's understanding of the logic of Aquinas' 'Five Ways', and in particular the second of those ways.

Herbert McCabe offers a reading of the Second Way which aspires to respect Thomas' pervasive awareness that God is not a god, not an entity amongst entities but rather utterly transcendent to the world He created: hence 'creation' cannot be understood as a kind of causation, since what we mean by 'causation' is essentially a transformative process, in which something is made to be or to be otherwise by means of something else operating either upon it or upon that from which it is made. At the same time, however, McCabe also wants to argue that our familiar ways of inquiring into worldly causes naturally and legitimately lead us from the domain in which the concept of 'causation' is at home to one in which we encounter the idea of God as Creator of all, as mysterious answer to the question 'Why something rather than nothing?'

McCabe presents this process as one of increasing depth or funda-mentality, or increasingly wide contextualization. We start with 'How come Fido is present in the world with us, as opposed to not being there?', a good answer to which might simply involve pointing out his canine parents; but insofar as that answer presupposes the existence of dogs as a species, we may naturally be led to ask 'How come there are such things as dogs?', to which an answer in terms of genetics and natural selection is no doubt available; but since any such answer presupposes the existence of a biological realm within which such processes operate, it too may naturally lead us to ask 'How come animals?', 'How come living things?', 'How come material things?', and so on until we reach the question 'How come something rather than nothing at all?'[1]

The questioning process that McCabe has in mind never loses its initial focus on Fido—it is always his existence in the world that we want to explain. But by placing him against increasingly broad or fundamental backgrounds we disclose more and more of what it is for him to be what he is, and so what it is that his canine parents brought about in bringing him into existence (for in bringing this particular dog into being, they brought into being—at least—a molecularly structured, biologically complex living member of the dog species); and at every level at which we pose one of this series of questions, we answer it by reference to some existing reality or state of affairs in virtue of which Fido is what he is as opposed to not being so (a dog as opposed to a cat, an animal as

[1] Cf. 'Creation', in his *God Matters* (London: Geoffrey Chapman, 1987).

opposed to a plant, animate as opposed to inanimate, etc). But when we reach the stage of asking 'How come Fido exists instead of nothing?', then the context in which we place him is nothing less than everything; we are asking not why Fido exists as opposed to not being a part of the world (which is where we started), but rather why he exists as opposed to there not being a world at all.

Here, however, a difficulty with McCabe's strategy appears to emerge: for at this point we seem to lose our grip on the 'alternative' that his question appears (like all its less radical *confrères*) to invoke. The 'alternative' to there being a world is not the world's being some other way but rather there being nothing at all; but we have no concept of nothing at all, of absolutely nothing (as opposed to there being nothing in the cupboard, or in some other given portion of space and time). And we simultaneously thereby deprive ourselves of any resource for answering this 'question', since in all of its less radical or all-embracing forms, that which we are attempting to account for is not everything, and so room is left to invoke something else that might account for it. Hence, insofar as we invoke 'God' as our 'answer' to this radical causal 'question', we must recognize that we cannot regard his role as Creator of the world as involving any familiar idea of causal power. To say that God created the world *ex nihilo* is precisely to deny that he caused or made it, since it explicitly denies that he transformed anything (given that the result of his creativity is everything, there could not be anything upon which he operated or out of which it came).

It may help to appreciate both the nature of this problem, and the difficulty of addressing it in a way which properly acknowledges its depth, if we turn here to the way in which it is confronted by a theologian who is (rightly) not numbered amongst the Grammatical Thomists, but whose treatment of Aquinas places him in surprisingly close intellectual proximity to them, and whose example can therefore serve as a useful warning of the dangers that threaten anyone attempting to chart a safe course through this intellectual terrain. Here is Denys Turner discussing divine causality in ways that seem remarkably reminiscent of McCabe:

'Nothing' . . . is not a peculiar sort of causally explanatory 'something' . . . neither is there some specialized theological sense which might give force to that sort of 'out of' which is 'out of nothing'; the 'ex' of 'ex nihilo' means, Thomas says, just the contrary: the negation negates the 'out of', no antecedent conditions, so no process, no event; an 'after', but no 'before'. It is just for this reason that the notion of a 'cause of everything' strains at the lines of continuity with our ordinary, intra-mundane, explanatory employments of cause. (FREG,[2] 251)

'Strains at', or breaks free of those moorings altogether? The adjectives with which Turner qualifies his reference to our ordinary employments of 'cause' imply a differently qualified alternative—a contrast between intra-mundane, explanatory employments of 'causes' and some other mode of its employment (presumably extra-mundane and non-explanatory?). But in fact, those adjectives merely bring out what many Wittgensteinians (Rundle and Kenny prominent amongst them) would call the ordinary grammar of 'cause'—elements in the pattern of its ordinary uses: all the uses of 'cause' with which we are familiar are explanatory and intra-mundane, because the very idea of an extra-mundane cause cancels itself out, as Turner has just pointed out (and claimed that Thomas points out). So the implied alternative use for the notion of cause (with respect to the world or everything) is in fact one in which our ordinary pattern of use is negated or cancelled in every respect, and no other pattern of use is supplied.

Turner is of course well aware of this:

The question arises as a causally explanatory question—it has grammatically the same shape that demands for an explanation of events in the world have—and to that extent the question retains its lines of continuity with all the causally explanatory questions which lead to it. But its logical oddity lies in its self-cancelling character: for we know...that the bringing about of anything 'out of nothing' cannot be any kind of causal *process* such that any kind of causal law governs it... Hence if in being a causal question, the answer to it must have the character of a cause, we have, in thus answering the question, lost control over the understanding of the causality involved. (FREG, 252)

Turner thinks that this combination of claims is coherent because he thinks we can distinguish a grasp of the causal nature of the question being posed from a grasp of the causality invoked in or as the answer to it. As he puts it a little later:

If [Thomas'] argument-strategy consists in the justification principally of a *question*—the question 'Why anything?'—then we can say that it is the question which lies on the 'inside' of language, and so of reason and so of logic, and it is the answer which must lie on the other side of all three. Hence while the question

---

[2] *Faith, Reason and the Existence of God* (Cambridge: Cambridge University Press, 2004), hereafter FREG.

retains its lines of continuity with our ordinary causal questions, the answer does not and could not do so. In short, the existence of God is in the nature of a demonstrated unknowability. *Et hoc omnes dicunt 'Deum'*. (FREG, 256)

Turner here resorts to a picture of language (and so of reason and of logic) as having an inside (within which the question is to be located) and another side or an outside (where the answer to the question must lie). To be sure, he does so in a highly dialectical manner (as part of an attempt to show how Thomas' argument-strategy escapes a particular dilemma), and his use of scare quotes betrays a certain unease about the terminology he thereby finds himself employing; but use it he neverthe-less does, and use it he apparently must because otherwise he cannot distinguish question from answer in the manner needed to rebut the charge that constructing proofs and acknowledging transcendence in this context are mutually exclusive. Unfortunately, there are good Witt-gensteinian reasons for questioning the legitimacy of this way of thinking about the limits of language.

For Rundle, Malcolm, and Diamond would all agree, first, that for the later Wittgenstein anything lying on 'the other side of' or 'outside' language could only be nonsense; and nonsense is not a peculiar (say, a peculiarly mysterious or ungraspable) kind of sense—it is the plain and simple absence of sense. The limits of sense are not limitations, bound-aries fencing us out from a domain of intelligibility that lies beyond mere humans; they mark the point at which meaning runs out. There is no outside to 'grammar' or 'logic'; hence, if the answer to the radical causal question lies on the other side of grammar or logic, it is not mysterious or ineffable but simply devoid of meaning or content—it merely appears to be meaningful. And if there is no outside to grammar or logic, then (second) there is no inside to it either; so to say that a causal question lies inside language could only amount to saying that it is a genuine, intel-ligible use of language—one that is not merely continuous with our everyday ways or kinds of questioning but a fully fledged instance of one of those kinds. And that, of course, is precisely *not* what Turner wishes to say about his question: although he does say that it 'arises as' or 'has the same shape as' a causal question, he never says that it *is* a causal question. And there are good reasons not to do so: for (third), if we have lost control of, lost our grip on, how the causality involved in our answer to this question is to be understood, how could we be confident that we retain our grip on the causality involved in posing the question?

We cannot, after all, grasp or pose that question unless we at least think it possible to specify what it is that stands in need of causal explanation— namely, 'anything whatever', the world or the universe, all that is; this, one might say, is (part of) what it is for that question to have the same grammatical shape as intra-mundane causal questions. But then, even to ask that question is to present oneself as capable of grasping 'the world', or 'anything whatever', as an intelligible object of causal explanation; and Turner has already acknowledged—even celebrated—the fact that 'any-thing whatever' is not a kind of thing, hence not the kind of thing that might be conceivable as the effect of some cause. If it were, its Creator would be conceivable as a cause, as a transformative or productive power: and that is precisely to render the answer to this 'question' as intelligible as the question itself (and thereby to render God as precisely not the begin-ning and end of all things, not what '*omnes dicunt "Deum"*').

If, by contrast, we take seriously the idea that we have lost our grip on what we might mean by saying that God creates *ex nihilo*, and further acknowledge that what we want to mean by 'the world' is essentially 'that which God creates *ex nihilo*', then what we mean by 'the world' is no more under our control than what we mean by 'creation *ex nihilo*'. But if that isn't under our control, then neither is the meaning of the question 'Why the world (or all that is, or anything whatever)?' In short: either the question is not the one to which 'God' is the (incomprehensible) answer, or we have lost control over what it might mean to ask it.

Could we rescue Turner's use of this picture by dispensing with talk of the inside and the outside of language, and instead making use only of the idea of its limits? We might, after all, quite naturally take his talk of his question's lines of continuity with explanatory causal questions as implying that it brings us to the limits of the intelligible—that it takes our ordinary notion of 'causal explanation' as far as it can possibly go without actually losing all sense. Of course, what this invocation of limits might amount to will differ according to whether one draws upon the early or the later Wittgenstein (and it is striking how far Tractarian turns of phrase and thought crop up in writings that have been taken to incorporate signature concepts of Wittgenstein's later work). But it is not obvious that either phase of Wittgenstein's thought is capable of providing what Turner needs at this point.

According to the *Tractatus*, whether or not one's reading of it is resolute, the limits of sense are articulated or made manifest by propositions of logic, which are not nonsensical but senseless, that is, degenerate propositions which are logically well-formed but whose mode of composition from elementary propositions is such as to cancel out their content. All tautologies say the same thing—because they all say precisely nothing; but since each possesses logical form, and the logical form of each can differ, then each can show something different (for example, that a given proposition is a tautology might show that a particular rule of inference is valid). This notion of the limits of sense fits Turner's picture in one way, since the idea of well formed but senseless propositions resonates with his idea that the radical causal question is continuous with ordinary ones by virtue of having the same shape (a matter of form rather than content). The problem is that, on the Tractarian view, these propositions show the limits of language precisely insofar as they say nothing whatever; so their continuity with senseful or intelligible propositions is purely formal, which means that it is not a matter of semantic content—*a fortiori* one involving the highly content-ful idea of 'intra-mundane' causes. Of course, as we have already seen, the *Tractatus* also offers a distinctive reading of mystical, ethico-religious language. But according to the standard reading of the book, it interprets them as nonsensical rather than senseless, that is as attempting to violate the limits of sense—to articulate a field of ineffable truths lying outside the grasp of language—rather than making those limits manifest; and I have already argued that this way of reading these stretches of the book is unfaithful to its basic vision of the relation between language and reality. So even if the standard reading of the *Tractatus* did provide a usable notion of the limits of sense, Turner wouldn't or shouldn't want it.

If he were instead to invoke the later Wittgenstein, then the obvious way of giving substance to the idea of the limits of sense would involve the notion of 'grammar'; indeed, grammatical remarks are often charac-terized as articulating a rule or norm governing our practice of employ-ing a word—hence a way of articulating what it makes sense to say. However, the normative significance of grammar is such as to render empty the idea that a grammatical remark itself advances a contentful claim. One might well argue that the apophatic dimension of Turner's account of Aquinas could be presented as a way of marking the limits of intelligible talk about 'God'—so that, for example, to say that God creates *ex nihilo* is simply to remind us that God cannot intelligibly be thought of as being or exercising a causal power. But to say that God is not a cause of any kind is then simply to say that causal talk when applied to God has not been assigned a sense—that it has no grammar; it is precisely not to say that, when employed to construct the radical causal question to which 'God' is the only possible answer, it has a grammar which is both essentially continuous with that governing its ordinary use and essentially discontinuous with it (at once pointing us in the direction of God's role as Creator and making manifest His incomprehensibility in any such terms). For that seems to amount to saying that the term both has a familiar grammatical shape and altogether lacks one; and that really doesn't sound like an intelligible way in which a word might have a grammar. Or must the grammar of the terms through which we reflect upon whether and how we can talk about God be just as mysterious as that to which they aspire impossibly to refer?

3.2 Wittgensteinian Worries about these Wittgensteinian Worries

I think that the answer to that last question is and must be 'Yes', and that any genuinely Wittgensteinian response to Grammatical Thomism ought to accept and defend it. One might think of the situation in the following way. Any inheritor of Wittgenstein's example in philosophy ought to acknowledge that the signature concepts with which Wittgensteinian work is so often identified ('language-game', 'grammar', 'forms of life') are representational devices intended simply to put things before us as they really are (as ways of ensuring that we look and see what is in front of our eyes despite our conviction that it must take a particular form (PI 66), of describing the very various ways language in fact works despite our urge to misunderstand them (PI, 109), of delineating the actual use of words exactly as it is without either interfering with it or attempting to justify it (PI, 124)). Wittgenstein took it that in many cases of philosophical confusion, we might alleviate our conflicted tendency to think that things must be a certain way whilst being unable to deny that they appeared for all the world to be otherwise if we were to ask ourselves how we actually used words in this vicinity; and such self-interrogation is very often facilitated by conceiving of our life with words in terms of language-games possessed of a grammatical structure and embodied in a specific form of life.

But if—like any other representational conventions—this set of signature concepts is sufficiently robust to acquire a life of its own, then they might on occasions stand between us and an ability simply to acknowledge how things really are; rather than helping to subvert our tendency towards the imposition of a philosophical 'must', they may actually subserve its further expression. And when a Wittgensteinian philosopher becomes so committed to the use of these signature concepts that he cannot conceive of another way of perspicuously representing the phenomena of our life with language when responding to a philosophical problem, then he has in effect imposed a set of philosophical preconditions on the reality he putatively aspires simply to describe. He has donned a set of Wittgensteinian conceptual spectacles; and by employing those concepts as lenses through which he views everything, he actively subverts the realistic spirit in which their creator forged and at least attempted to deploy them.

Deep issues arise from this way of picturing possible conflicts between the realistic spirit of Wittgenstein's philosophy and the signature concepts through which he gave expression to it; and I shall return to them in later lectures. But the immediate value of outlining the matter in this way is that it allows us to understand the difficulty posed for Wittgensteinians by Grammatical Thomism. For every Wittgensteinian (such as Bede Rundle or Norman Malcolm) for whom Wittgenstein's concept of 'grammar' provides a stable and essentially non-controversial or undogmatic lens through which to describe the phenomena of our life with religious language and reveal when our uses of words only appear to have an intelligible use, there is a Wittgensteinian (such as Cora Diamond) for whom the undeniable fact that some of us are inclined to use words in distinctively religious ways provides us with an opportunity to acknowledge that our purportedly uncontroversial concept of 'grammar' here risks preventing us from seeing what is really in front of our eyes. So the question arises: is a Grammatical Thomist account of how talk about God functions an account of one more way in which we can delude ourselves into thinking that we are talking sense, or is it rather an account of one more way in which we really can mean what we say? Have the Grammatical Thomists delineated the mere appearance of a grammar, or an actual grammar that shows up the incipient dogmatism of one familiar Wittgensteinian conception of grammar?

We can clarify what is at stake here by recalling Turner's claim that the radical causal question lies inside language, whilst its answer lies on the other side of language. I've already articulated a standard Wittgenstein-ian objection to this kind of claim—one which turns on the counter-claim that it is part of the grammar of a 'question' that anyone in a position to pose a question must by that very token grasp what might in principle count as an answer to it. But is that claim as undogmatic as it is meant to be? Or rather: if we gloss that claim in a way which makes it no more than a grammatical reminder, just what limits are we justified in placing on what counts as 'grasping what might count as an answer to a question'? My suggestion is that (pace the usual Thomist disdain for Anselmian ontological proofs) Diamond's treatment of Anselm is preg-nant with possibilities for reorienting our Wittgensteinian evaluation of the strategies of Grammatical Thomism around just this hinge or pivot.

Suppose we try thinking of the Thomists' radical causal question as a great riddle—thereby deriving a rather different tuition from Turner's intuition that it has the shape of a causal question. Like Anselm's riddle phrase, it is constructed by extending a sequence of ordinary causal questions ordered as a series of increasing generality or fundamentality; like all riddles, it has such sense as we are inclined to attribute to it by virtue of our familiarity with the concepts and procedures of causal explanation on analogy with which it has been constructed; and on that same basis, we impose conditions on the kind of answer to the question that we are willing to accept—in particular, we exclude a range of possible answers (by, for example, concluding that the creator of everything cannot possess or instantiate a kind of causal power).

The power of Diamond's analogy between theological language and riddle phrases is not restricted to this particular passage, however. On the contrary, if we are willing to consider such a treatment of the Second Way as exemplary, it invites us to view the whole of Aquinas' project in the Summa as generated by a willingness to respond positively and creatively to the enigmatic authority of one particular riddling phrase from scripture—one amongst many scriptural and doctrinal shapes of truth that Aquinas treats as divinely authorized or inspired acts of speech, hence as aspects of God's revelation of himself to us, but which therefore necessarily present themselves to us as inherently mys-terious or enigmatic. This anchoring phrase is introduced very early in Aquinas' treatment of his first Question, 'the nature and scope of sacred

doctrine': having argued that we required instruction from divine revelation not only to supplement the disclosures of human reason, but also
to place reason's deliverances in the right light, in Article 3 he goes on to
offer his first characterization of God's presentation of Himself in sacred
scripture and doctrine: 'Sacred doctrine...is chiefly concerned with
God, and it turns to creatures considered as being in relation to him,
their origin and end' (1a.1, 3, ad 1[3]).

This last phrase is reiterated in Article 7, as the primary mode in which
God appears as the subject of the science of theology: 'sacred doctrine
deals with all things in terms of God, either because they are God himself
or because they are related to him as their origin and end'. And the
scriptural basis for such a characterization of God is to be found in
passages such as the following, from the Book of Revelation (22:13): 'I am
Alpha and Omega, the beginning and the end, the first and the last.'

In effect, then, the opening Question which orients the whole of the
Summa project (with its tripartite structure embodying a vision of all
reality as flowing from and eventually returning to its divine source)
takes its bearings in turn from that Biblical phrase—treating it as its own
alpha and omega. But Aquinas need not be read as taking its meaning to
be obvious or transparent, a familiar part of the grammar of homely
religious language-games about which we need only to be reminded. We
might rather interpret the rest of the *Summa* as an attempt to make such
sense of that enigmatic phrase as is possible, given the concepts and
procedures that are available to us for doing so. The claim that God is the
beginning and end of all things is a riddle phrase, an element of sacred
scripture that Aquinas takes to crystallize the basic revelation of the
whole body of divinely inspired texts; so he devotes his commentary to
the task of forging or working out the promise of necessary connections
between this original phrase and as many as possible of the other riddling
shapes of truth bequeathed to us by scripture and tradition. He thereby
constructs or projects the 'grammar' of a 'language' whose adequacy to
the divine reality is guaranteed by the authority of its source, but which
we are not and cannot be in a position simply to speak or mean. We
understand it as much and as little as we understand the auxiliary

---

[3] All quotations from the *Summa* are taken from the translation in *Summa Theologiae:
Questions on God*, ed. B. Davies and B. Leftow (Cambridge: Cambridge University Press,
2006).

conditions we construct and impose on the correct solution to a riddle or the development of a proof of a mathematical conjecture: in other words, we understand *that* God is the solution to all the riddles out of which this 'language' has been woven or knitted, but not how he is.

We can then think of the Five Ways (those opening elements of Aquinas' response to his second Question) as his initial attempt to impose conditions on the kind of solution to that riddle that we might be willing to accept. If we are willing to call anything 'the beginning and end of all things', would we be willing to call it a thing—an object, a substance, an individual particular? Well: according to Thomas' best understanding of thinghood, any thing is alterable, capable of causing alteration in other things only insofar as it is capable of being made subject to their causal efficacy, capable of going out of existence, imperfect and capable of being subject to the goal-directedness of others. In one sense, therefore, the realm of things gives content to the very idea of 'beginnings' and 'ends' out of which the riddle phrase is constructed: without a grasp of alteration and its causes, contingent as opposed to necessary existence, and the way in which values can function as standards and goals, and so bring things and activities into being for the sake of fulfilling an end, we would have no initial grip on the riddle phrase at all. But precisely because that initial grasp of beginning and ending is conditioned by its applicability to things amidst other things (that is, as part of a system or world in which what alters or destroys a thing, what shows it to be lacking or puts it to goal-directed use, is some other thing), appreciating that fact has two consequences. First, it naturally generates the impulse to put together the ideas of beginning and ending in a less conditioned or relative way; to construct the concept of something that is (not the beginning or ending—whether causal or teleological—of some particular thing or things but) the beginning and end of all things. And second, it entails that anything answering to that description could not itself be a thing: for if it were, then some other thing could in principle constitute its beginning or end. Accordingly, whilst we couldn't have constructed the idea of 'the beginning and end of all things' except out of our conception of what it is to be a thing amongst other things, that point of origin at once implants a natural projective trajectory for the relevant expressions and excludes the possibility that whatever answers to the resulting linguistic construction (what fulfils the intellectual desire articulated thereby) could be any such thing.

If 'the beginning and end of all things' cannot be a thing, then it cannot have the ontological profile of a thing. And the Five Ways implicitly spell out what Aquinas takes to be the crucial aspects or dimensions of that ontology: the distinction between matter and form (integral to the First and Second Ways), the distinction between essence and existence (implicit in the Third Way), and the distinction between a thing's present actualization of the norms and ends internal to its nature and the fullest possible such realization (invoked in the Fourth and Fifth Ways). We might call these elaborations of our core conception of what it is for a thing to have a nature, a particular manner or mode of being; they also display that and how any given thing is necessarily open to other things (necessarily capable of variously affecting and being affected by them) in the system of nature. If such divisions or diremptions—such structural multiplicities—are internal to thinghood, then 'the beginning and end of all things' must lack them: where things suffer a kind of non-self-identity, one might say, 'the beginning and end of all things' must be genuinely self-identical—wholly one, absolutely simple.

Here, the process of constructing the conditions that must be satisfied by anything answering to this riddle phrase makes contact with another Biblical riddle phrase—one that Aquinas cites immediately before developing his Five Ways, at the outset of Article 3: 'Exodus represents God as saying "I am who I am"' (Exodus 3:14). This great tautology immediately denies that, with respect to the beginning and end of all things, one could make a distinction between essence and existence; but since such a denial cannot be carried through without simultaneously denying the applicability of the distinction between form and matter or between *telos* and actuality, it confirms what our imaginative conjecture based on the riddle phrase from Revelation independently displays—divine simplicity. And this is the insight from which Aquinas begins in his third Question—the insight which orients the rest of his treatment of our ability to know and name God in the *Summa*.

David Burrell formulates Aquinas' way of formulating the Exodus tautology as follows: 'to be God is to be to-be'; or, slightly more telegraphically: 'to be God is to be'. And it is precisely this kind of formulation that, as we saw in Lecture One, draws the most extreme criticism from Wittgensteinians such as Kenny and Rundle: each in their different ways makes it clear that they find it hard to imagine anything more radically absurd or lacking in sense, complete nonsense (Kenny), or sheer defiance of grammar (Rundle). But what Diamond's analogy between religious discourse and riddles allows us to appreciate is that sheer nonsensicality is precisely the point. The radical causal question of the Second Way, or the Five Ways taken as a whole, or the Biblical phrases that orient Aquinas' treatment from its outset, are exemplary instances of a great riddle; and what distinguishes great riddles from mere or simple riddles, like that confronted by the princess who is told to come to the ball neither clothed nor unclothed, is that an intelligible answer to them is not just a leap of the imagination away (as it is for the princess, who attends the ball wearing a fishing net). On the contrary, their significance for us as questions is crucially dependent on the fact that we exclude *a priori* the possibility that we might construct or come upon a satisfactory answer to them out of our own resources.

Take the Second Way: one might say that just as divine Creation *ex nihilo* is necessarily not a kind of human creative activity, the very meaning of the word 'Creation' in this context is necessarily not the result of human linguistic creativity. From the point of view of any intellectually consistent religious believer on Aquinas' view of the matter, the meaning of that phrase can only be given to us, and by the very Being to whom it will at last successfully refer (when and only when we meet Him face to face); and one way of expressing that conviction is to refuse to accept any proffered specification of a grammar for these words, precisely on the grounds that doing so would confer intelligibility upon them. Faith herewith finds a use for nonsense that is significantly different from the (primarily ethical) one we explored in the *Tractatus* and the Grimm's fairy tales, and yet not unrelated to it.

Diamond herself sees this point as being grammatically (or rather, 'grammatically') related to the Christian idea of God as a God of revelation—as having revealed Himself, in deed and word (those of His prophets and, in the Christian case, those of Christ himself), and as having thereby made it possible for His hearers to speak and act in response to this unprecedented self-revelation.[4] It is only in the terms made newly available through God's actions in history that the hearer can understand those actions, and their source, as divine: God Himself has thereby given a transformed content to the word 'God'. Diamond,

---

[4] Cf. her essay 'Wittgenstein and Religious Belief: The Gulfs between Us', in D.Z. Phillips and M. von der Ruhr (eds), *Religion and Wittgenstein's Legacy* (London: Ashgate, 2005).

following Rosenzweig, calls this the conversion of our concepts through God's self-revelation.

An orthodox Wittgensteinian philosopher such as Phillips will happily note that this religious believer describes her language-game as one in which God speaks and is responded to; but (as we saw in Lecture One) he will naturally ask what, in her game, counts as God's having spoken— what the grammatical criteria are that she and her fellow believers employ in playing this language-game. From the believer's point of view, however, the very form of that question implies that we—in our ways of speaking—are the ones who ultimately determine what counts as God's speaking; whereas it is essential to her understanding of the God of whom she speaks that her ways with religious words have a kind of openness to God's actions, an openness which means that it is not for her (or anyone other than God himself) to lay down rules for what counts as God's speaking. To do otherwise would mean arrogating to ourselves the authority to determine the limits of God's capacity to reveal himself, rather than remaining open to the possibility that his self-revelation might show up our current ways of talking about him as utterly shallow or misconceived.

The picture of God as speaking is thus not only central to the religious language-games that she plays but also to the way she regards or relates to those language-games—namely, not as practices in which what counts as God's speaking is ultimately subject to determination by our rules. She will therefore resist any philosophical description of her religious language that makes its deployment ultimately a matter of our modes of speaking rather than God's. In Tractarian terms, such descriptions give expression to the philosopher's unhappiness, his unwillingness to acknowledge reality's independence of human attempts to determine its possible limits. In Kierkegaardian terms, one might more positively say that the religious believer's relation to her religious discourse exemplifies that of the knight of faith. Her words must be treasured as having the immeasurable value accruing to any gift from God, as embodying the impossible but undeniable actuality of his revelation of himself to us in all his absolute otherness; but her relation to them (like Abraham's to Isaac) properly expresses that value only if she cleaves to them whilst being always already willing to renounce them (for example, in the light of further divine self-revelation), thereby giving expression to her continuing awareness of his inexhaustible transcendence. But however we articulate the matter, any Wittgensteinian commitment to eliciting the grammar of her ways of speaking, where the relevant criteria are taken to be hers or her tradition's to determine and employ, will misrepresent that way of speaking. This signature Wittgensteinian concept will here prevent us from simply acknowledging the reality of what lies before us, unless one radically recasts an aspect of its normal grammar that one might hitherto have taken to be uncontroversially essential to it.

The perspective of religious faith embodies conceptions of meaning, hence of logic and of rationality, that are not only specific to it but partly constitutive of that particular form of life with language. Even the most seemingly innocuous or minimal forms of philosophical presumption about the phenomena of meaning and reason risk occluding fundamental features of certain instances of the very subject matter that Wittgensteinians aspire simply to acknowledge. This, I take it, is why, when McCabe attempts to explain the conception of word meaning that underlies a Thomist view of language in relation to God, he treats words as analogous to any other element of God's Creation:

St. Thomas thought that things in some way pointed beyond themselves to something which is not a thing, which is altogether outside the universe of things and cannot be included in any classification with them. Given this idea, it is not too difficult to understand his notion that words can point beyond their ordinary meanings, and this he thought is what happens when we talk about God. We can use words to mean more than we can understand ... the meaning of the words—what controls our use of them—is their meaning in application to creatures. When we use them of God we are trying to mean more than this ... [we] are not straying outside [their] normal meaning but trying to enter more deeply into it. (KNG,[5] 104-7)

The picture is one according to which words point beyond themselves in just the way that all created things do: it is part of the gift of their own nature that the maximal realization of that nature amounts to its self-transcendence. On the Thomist account, word meaning is ultimately kenotic or self-emptying: it has a fundamentally sacramental or Christological form.

The structural or grammatical resemblance here between a Thomist treatment of religious language and Wittgenstein's treatment of

---

[5] Appendices 2 and 3, *Summa Theologiae*, vol. 3 (1a. 12–13), *Knowing and Naming God*, trans. H. McCabe (Cambridge University Press: Cambridge, 2006), hereafter KNG.

ethico-religious discourse in the *Tractatus* is striking and suggestive. In both cases, we find the human imagination committed to the construction of a form of words that extrapolates everyday speech patterns to the point at which they become utterly severed from their original contexts, and to valuing the result of that construction process precisely because of its lack of sense. We find ourselves exploiting grammatical continuities or analogies in the service of marking a radical discontinuity, and discovering that only a refusal to accept any clear assignment of sense to these words will reflect the significance they have for us. Our purposes would not be served by any old signs deprived of sense in any old way—by any words whatever, provided only that they lack a determinate use. On the contrary, these pieces of nonsense have the significance they do for us only because they result from an imaginative operation of a very particular kind on precisely these words—words with this particular kind of everyday use, hence unmoored from these particular kinds of context, and unmoored by way of what we naturally think of as an intensification of their ordinary sense-bearing features. We negate their sense in a highly determinate way, by exploiting one dimension of their projective potential—one particular aspect of their ineliminable capacity to project themselves beyond any given range of contexts of use. Only by so doing could our refusal to accept any assignment of sense to them in their unmoored state simultaneously signify something determinate—call it an openness to transcendence rather than to anything whatever (which would mean to nothing whatever); only thus could we feel that such projections of them are also disclosures of the mysterious essence that underlies their ordinary uses.

As with his treatment of the Second Way, Denys Turner's attempt to articulate Aquinas' conception in terms of reason rather than language comes very close to the Grammatical Thomist position, but without quite arriving at a fully stable formulation of it. Here is how he puts his view of Thomas' vision:

[The shape of reason] is determined by an interplay between the cataphatic and the apophatic, between word and silence, which also determines the shape of faith. The question 'cataphatically' asks, and 'God' is given to the question as its 'apophatic' answer. More specifically, the shape of reason is 'incarnational', and it is so precisely in that exercise of reason in which, at the end of its tether, it reaches that question it can ask, though it cannot take hold of the mystery which answers to it... [This is] the 'proto-sacramentality' of reason. (FREG, 256–7)

The ideas of reason as incarnational, and of the essential interplay of cataphatic and apophatic in the notion of creation *ex nihilo*, seem exactly right; but Turner once again succumbs to the temptation of sharply distinguishing between the question and its answer, so that the former (being inside language) is all cataphatic and the latter (being outside it) is all apophatic—quite as if the interplay takes place between question and answer, rather than being equally at work in both (insofar as the question takes the form of a riddle).

A theologian closer to McCabe's understanding of the matter might rather say: ethico-religious language of this kind is at once cataphatical and apophatical, or rather its being apophatical is a matter of its being determinately non-cataphatical, of its negating cataphatically determinate uses of language. Indeed, one might well think of Denys Turner's earlier treatment of mysticism in *The Darkness of God* as summarizable in just those terms, or at least a variant upon them.[6] For on that account, insofar as God is the source of all that is, possessing in his being all the perfections he causes, then everything in creation is a potential source of imagery for the divine, and the more of it we activate in religious language the better, since only thus can we acknowledge God's superabundant variety. And yet, using language in all these ways simultaneously will inevitably lead to us speaking contradictorily about God (as male and female, light and darkness, weakness and strength); and nothing we say about him can conceivably capture his nature anyway. But that transcendence of God is best acknowledged precisely by following out the consequences of attributing contradictory attributes to him; for if he is both male and female, and we know that no person can be both male and female, we thereby appreciate that our idea of him as a personal God is itself a misrepresentation—a necessarily unsuccessful attempt to delineate that which is beyond delineation.

The best way to appreciate the transcendence of God to human language is thus not to fall into silence, avoiding even the assertion that nothing is assertable of him, or to attempt some inconceivable synthesis of affirmation and negation; it is rather endlessly to employ that language in relation to him, and endlessly to experience its inevitable collapse upon itself. Religious language is thus essentially self-subverting language; the

---

[6] Cf. *The Darkness of God* (Cambridge: Cambridge University Press, 1995).

repeated collapse of its affirmations into complete disorder *is* its mode of order—it is, one might say, the only way the 'language-games' woven into honest, transparent religious language-games should be played.

Can a Wittgensteinian philosopher allow himself to acknowledge religious language in such terms? Perhaps a better question to ask is: can any philosopher attempting to inherit the realistic spirit of Wittgenstein's thinking really have grounds for refusing to take religious language seriously on these terms, if they can be made out to be the terms that reflective religious believers themselves find apt? In Lecture Four I will begin to map out some of the lessons that might be drawn (by Wittgensteinians and others) from the examples of language use upon which and with which Aquinas reflects—lessons concerning the nature of word meaning, of human understanding, and of philosophical investigation itself.

Lecture Four

Analogical Uses and the Projectiveness of Words
Wittgenstein's Vision of Language

In Lecture Three, I argued that light might be cast both on Aquinas and on the Wittgensteinian legitimacy of the Grammatical Thomist reading of Aquinas if we took seriously the following idea: that there are humanly significant uses of language, constructed on the basis of familiar patterns of word use and ways of extending such patterns, whose point for those employing them lies precisely in the fact that any assignment of sense to them would frustrate their aims in constructing them. To find room for such a phenomenon would allow us to locate something of value in both of the two opposed modes of inheriting Wittgenstein for the philosophy of religion that I earlier distinguished, and hence to reject the sufficiency of either mode taken on its own: for the basic strategy is that of attending to the particular role played by such words in a form of life (as Phillips and Malcolm recommend), but identifying that role involves a willingness to regard the words so employed as devoid of sense (as Kenny and Rundle insist).

This conjunction of intelligible beginnings or origins and unintelligible ends or outcomes is bound to cause some intellectual difficulty. In Wittgensteinian terms, it appears to deny the truism that those words must either make sense (in which case they are housed in honest, transparent language-games, whether one or many) or make no sense at all (that is, have no such home or *Heimat*); in terms more familiar to Aquinas, and more specific to theology and religion, it appears to deny that words directed at God must be dismissed as useless unless they are used univocally or equivocally. And yet, neither mode of sense-making appears tempting in a religious context: if, for example, our talk of God as

Creator were univocal with our talk of sublunary causes, then his transcendence would be denied, but if it were equivocal with respect to such familiar talk, then we would need to specify the meaning particular to religious uses of these words (and so gain an understanding which has the effect of returning us to the first difficulty, by obliterating God's transcendence). But if these terms when employed religiously have a meaning that is neither univocal nor equivocal, then what on earth is their state or condition?

The apparent need for some third category of meaning tends to encourage commentators to expect great things when—in his treatment of Question 13—Aquinas invokes an idea of analogical usage. But it is a further distinctive feature of the Grammatical Thomist project that its proponents not only do not provide any systematic theory of analogy, but believe that Thomas himself had no particular interest in doing so either—that his goals were much more limited and indeed predominantly negative. As McCabe puts it: 'St. Thomas wishes to break down this either-or. It is not true that a word must mean either exactly the same in two different uses or else mean something altogether different. There is the possibility of a word being used with related meanings' (KNG, App. 4)—a possibility that Aquinas and McCabe both distinguish from metaphorical uses of words. Thus the point of citing there Aquinas' two famous instances of analogous usage—the use of the term 'healthy' of human beings and diet, and of diet and complexion, respectively—is simply to deprive those eager to create a dilemma of the means with which to do so. It is not the exemplary basis for a systematic explanation of how it is possible for words successfully to latch on to divine reality (perhaps by developing theories of attributive and proportional analogy): it is rather an attempt to subvert the compulsoriness of a picture according to which any two non-metaphorical uses of a word must be either absolutely identical or absolutely distinct.

Anyone committed to that picture might accordingly defend it in two ways: by regarding analogous usage as a species of univocal use, or by regarding it as a minor and eccentric exception to that general condition. Grammatical Thomists must therefore contest both defensive strategies: they must reject treatments of analogous usage which purportedly reveal them to be implicitly univocal, *and* treatments that render them utterly distinct from ordinary (non-analogous, non-metaphorical—call them generic) uses of words. For as we saw at the end of Lecture Three, what the

Grammatical Thomists find in religious uses of language is not solely or simply *sui generis*; it is also a revelation of something essential to the everyday words upon which the violently transfigurative religious impulse operates, and so a revelation of something fundamental to language as such (what McCabe calls the capacity of words to point beyond themselves).

4.1 Analogy and (Dis-)proportion: Mathematical Sources and Models

My major concern in this lecture is to suggest ways in which that more generally revelatory function of analogous uses of words might be taken as congenial rather than antithetical to a Wittgensteinian view of language. Before beginning that task, however, it is worth dwelling briefly on the first mode of resistance I mentioned—treating analogous uses as a species of univocal use. This is because an illuminating and sophisticated recent philosophical treatment of the concept of analogy in religion (by Roger M. White, in *Talking About God*[1]) presents David Burrell's critique of this strategy as plainly erroneous—despite the fact that Burrell himself thinks that he is simply repeating an argument so widely accepted amongst commentators at the time (1973) as to risk making its reiteration otiose.

Burrell is concerned with the highly influential Thomist tradition of interpreting analogical predication as captured by the structure of the mathematical concept of proportion, $a : b :: c : d$. In this tradition, exemplified by Cajetan, that mathematical schema is employed as an algorithmic device for normalizing analogous usage; and Burrell's criticism of it is quoted *in extenso* by White:

Thus 'good' said of a citizen and a train robbery is justified by recourse to the paradigm $a : b :: c : d$—'good : citizen :: good : robbery'—which reminds us strongly of $2 : 4 :: 3 : 6$. Now the mathematical example is useful to clarify what language leaves ambiguous: $good_1$—said of a citizen, must be distinguished from $good_2$—said of the robbery. For generally, if b differs from d, so must a from c if we are to preserve a proportion. Yet from this point on mathematical proportion ceases to be useful and becomes misleading. For ordered couples can be unequivocally expressed—in our case as $1 : 2$—and so form equalities: $2 : 4 = 3 : 6$. But all attempt to find an element (like the $1 : 2$) common to the ratios 'good : citizen' and 'good : robbery' have failed. Such efforts must fail since the very search for a

[1] Farnham: Ashgate, 2010, hereafter TAG.

schema to regularize the usage of terms like good sprang initially from want of a formula to express the conditions for their use. This failure to conform to an account which will not vary from one context to another is precisely what merits such terms being classified ... 'analogous'. So the commentary must point out that the '::' relating a:b with c:d may not be interpreted as '=', and this discrepancy signals the limits of any promise of systematic clarity. Since we know how to operate with = but have no idea what to do with ::, the schema a:b::c:d becomes itself an analogy, at once useful and misleading, for analogous usage. (APL,[2] 10)

White thinks that this passage is 'completely misguided':

We can see that he must have gone astray, since if his argument were good, it would rule out not only the problem cases such as the word 'good' but also the unproblematic cases of words said by analogy such as 'wing' said of birds and of butterflies.

Burrell's thought seems to be that people who have thought that a word like 'good' was said by analogy were claiming that there were different sorts of good, and that this good was to citizens as that good was to train robberies. That way of interpreting the claim does indeed lead to virtually unintelligible results. But this is not what Aristotle or Archytas had in mind .... the idea was not that there were different sorts of calm and that this calm was to the sea as that calm was to the air. The idea was, rather, that because windlessness was to the air as wavelessness was to the sea, we could use this analogy to introduce a concept, *calm*, which covered both these cases. When we compare Burrell's account with what Archytas did, we can see where Burrell has gone wrong. When we introduce a concept F, and say that the word 'F' that designates that concept is said by analogy, we do not use the word 'F' in the specification of the underlying analogical scheme. If we were to attempt to apply the analogy in the way suggested by Burrell, the circularity in the account would inevitably result in the kind of unintelligibility that he finds. (TAG, 174–5)

It is hard to know where to begin to set White right here; but his misapprehensions are rooted in the fact that he mistakenly regards the attempt to deploy mathematical proportion to elucidate analogous uses of language as Burrell's own rather than as the object of his critique. Using mathematical proportion in this way is not Burrell's thought or suggestion: it is Cajetan's, or rather Cajetan's suggestion for interpreting Aquinas; so given that White acknowledges that any such attempt would inevitably result in the kind of unintelligibility that Burrell claims to find, he unwittingly concedes the legitimacy of Burrell's primary critical point.

---

[2] *Analogy and Philosophical Language* (New Haven, CT: Yale University Press, 1973), hereafter APL.

Furthermore, since Burrell doesn't claim that Cajetan's view is that of Aristotle or Archytas (Burrell's treatment of Aristotle—whether or not he is as influenced by Archytas as White believes—comes much later, and is conducted in very different terms), then the fact that Burrell's Cajetan does not do what Archytas and Aristotle did cannot constitute a distinct critical point against Burrell. As for the idea that Burrell thinks that any and all 'people who have thought that a word like "good" was said by analogy' meant by that what Cajetan meant by that: the whole point of Burrell's project is to make a sharp distinction between Cajetan's gloss on that thought and other available glosses, whether philosophical, theological, or simply implicit in our everyday command of words.

Could we concede all this, and nevertheless sustain White's suspicions about Burrell's approach by interpreting them as directed against what he sees as Burrell's unduly narrow or impoverished conception of what might be drawn from the use of mathematical proportion as a paradigm for understanding analogous uses of words? White's general account certainly shows how the initial Greek conception of mathematical proportion was itself subject to rich and fruitful development; and a highly simplified summary of that illuminating account might run as follows.

The basic Pythagorean theory of commensurable geometrical magnitudes was extended to incorporate incommensurable geometrical magnitudes by specifying the relevant relation indirectly—that is, not by giving the value of A/B in such cases but by specifying the conditions under which the value of that ratio was identical to the value of another ratio C/D. But the Euclidean definitions that govern and encapsulate this insight could be extended beyond the domain of geometry to any kind of extensive magnitude whatever—not just space or volume, but also times, numbers, and so on. So extended, they articulate a concept of magnitude about which theorems can be established that would not need to be re-established for each specific mode of magnitude, but could nevertheless be applied to each by analogy. Then the principle that analogies alternate (i.e. that if $A:B::C:D$ then $A:C::B:D$) could itself be extended in its application, opening up the possibility that two ratios or proportions each holding within a different category or kind might, once related to one another, licence the construction of intrinsically cross-categorical concepts. This is what happens when the concept of velocity, understood as a ratio of distance over time, is constructed by alternation from the comparison of the ratios of two temporal magnitudes with two magnitudes of length. And if this can be done with categorically distinct mathematical kinds or domains, why not extend the process, *mutatis mutandis*, to non-mathematical ones?

White also tells a parallel story about the idea of analogical modelling, which finds its core mathematical expression in Euclid's proportional conception of one figure being a scale model of another, thereby licensing such analogical inferences as, for example, that their corresponding angles will be identical. This opens up the possibility of arguments from analogy from models of any kind—whether specifically non-geometrical mathematical ones or non-mathematical ones—to their originals (provided only that the relevant properties prove invariant under analogy).

It is the fruitful possibilities inherent in extending both of these lines of development to the non-mathematical realm that White thinks are first realized in the work of Archytas and Aristotle; so he is naturally inclined to think that anyone who dismisses mathematical proportion as a paradigm for understanding analogous uses of words is dismissing those possibilities, and so dismissing the legitimacy of the patterns of word use that they may illuminate. But White himself seems oblivious of one crucial feature of his own genealogy of mathematical proportion: although each step in its development results in the construction of a new mathematical technique or proof-system, the developmental process itself is not a matter of applying such a technique or making a move in such a system. Each step is engendered not by the mechanical application of a formula but by the imaginative projection of an existing formulaic pattern into a new context—by analogy, as it were. The Pythagorean conception of commensurable geometrical proportion is an analogical model for its mathematical and non-mathematical successors, just as the Euclidean idea of a scale model itself engenders analogically a more general idea of analogical modelling, and of argument by analogy.

Now look at the paragraph immediately following the one White quotes from Burrell, in which Burrell picks up the thought that 'the schema $a:b::c:d$ becomes itself an analogy, at once useful and misleading, for analogous usage':

The circularity, nevertheless, is vitiating only for those who make formal or systematic claims for the schema. In such cases 'analogy' *will not work*. But once having made it, we see the limits of this retort. It is directed against a doctrine of analogy which courts systematic promise and offers the proportionality as a paradigm or normal form of analogous discourse. Should we, however, consider the schema rather as a model, looking to it more for illustration and understanding than for justification, we will no longer expect it to work in a systematic way. Yet it might nonetheless prove useful.

Of course, by invoking the schema as a model, we also open the way to different styles of 'analogy'. While a canonical form is by definition unique and looks quite definitive, we think more easily of alternative models. The project itself of putting ambiguities to work, however, seems to merit a single name. And 'analogy' has certainly come to be used in just this way: to refer to a project rather than a doctrine or canonized set of procedures. Harnessing ambiguities to systematic service requires a skill and a know-how that can be acquired only within a particular domain of discourse. Yet the very fruitfulness of the enterprise invites an investigation sensitive to the myriad ways we shape and use our language, while on the lookout for enough similarity to warrant the common name. (APL, 11)

I shall return to the reflexive implications of the second paragraph in Lecture Five; but the first paragraph suggests that a Burrellian response to White's account would involve two major points, one positive and one negative. The positive point is that, insofar as the use White makes of the concept of mathematical proportion is non-formulaic or-algorithmic—say, non-mathematical—then its basic strategy would be entirely consonant with that of Burrell's; for he too plainly sees nothing awry with the idea that that concept might prove a useful analogical model for helping us understand analogical uses of language.

The negative point concerns White's attempt to regard theological language in the light of the concept-formation process he sees exemplified in the already cited case of 'calm'. That concept, he tells us, is introduced on the basis of recognizing a cross-categorical analogy between two proportions: that of windlessness to the air and that of wavelessness to the sea. So far so good: but if this kind of analogical concept formation is White's preferred paradigm for theological language, then it carries rather more risks, and conveys rather less illumination, than he appears to think. For if, as he acknowledges, God cannot coherently be thought of as falling under any genus or category whatsoever (on pain of denying his transcendence), then how can a process of cross-categorical concept formation be used as a model for extending language from the categorical realm to the beginning and end of all things, the Creator of all that is, that than which nothing greater can be conceived? Modelling the relation between the realm of the categorical and that of the supra-categorical on that of any species of cross-categorical relation confronts us with a dilemma. Either it commits us to treating God's transcendence of all categories as if it were a kind of category—as if his incommensurability with the categorical as such were essentially commensurate with categorical incommensurabilities, and so indirectly specifiable in just the way cross-categorical relations are indirectly specifiable; or it forces us to employ exactly the linguistic move whose coherence it aspires to validate.

Burrell would not be made anxious by that latter circularity, which he takes to be ineliminable, and vitiating only if one proposes to make formal or systematic claims for the schema; but White's *modus operandi* seems reluctant to dispense altogether with such algorithmic aspiration. More charitably put: since he sees extra-mathematical analogical uses as deeply indebted to (and to that extent continuous with) mathematical ones, everything hangs on how he understands the way in which Pythagorean conceptions of relating commensurable magnitudes engender their mathematical and non-mathematical analogues. Is it by a process of concept formation that is itself generated and controlled mathematically (systematically or algorithmically), or is it rather a matter of analogy? Accordingly, much hangs on one's view of the ways in which mathematical proof systems are extended, in which new techniques and propositions are linked to existing ones; in short, we find ourselves yet again in the vicinity of mathematical conjectures.

4.2 Analogy, Projectibility, and Relatedness of Meaning

So much for resisting univocal treatments of analogical usage—the first of the necessary contestations I mentioned earlier. What of the second: resisting treatments of non-analogical (call them ordinary, or generic) uses of words as essentially discontinuous with analogical ones? If we ignore the spirit of McCabe's observation that words are not always either univocal or equivocal, since they can also have related meanings, we might simply assume that related meanings presuppose meanings to relate, and so think of analogous uses as a kind of compound or aggregate of distinct univocal uses (as if they were essentially another species of equivocation). We might also feel invited to think of non-analogous uses as univocal, where univocality is understood as essentially other than, even antithetical to, relatedness of meanings.

The Wittgensteinian analogue of such a literal-minded reading is one in which the unity of an ordinary language-game has one primary form (according to which its distinctive identity is capturable in a particular set of grammatical rules), from which it follows that the relations between distinct language-games (governed as they are by distinct sets of such rules) must be essentially external. Hence if a word is used in two different language-games, then it has two distinct meanings, and so the use of the same word in both games risks hiding a kind of ambiguity or equivocality: hence the key therapeutic response to philosophical confusion is to make these latent grammatical differences manifest. This is one tempting picture of how Wittgensteinian grammar and the therapy that its elucidation allows must be employed: a Wittgensteinian therapeutic response to it of the kind that I prefer, and that I believe is better suited to Grammatical Thomist purposes, will involve not replacing it by another, perhaps more sophisticated or even radically different one, but rather by removing our sense of its compulsoriness.

David Burrell's treatment of this matter is more extensive and so more nuanced than McCabe's lapidary formulation, but leaves itself equally open to misinterpretation. Here is his initial characterization of analogous uses of language:

[A]nalogous expressions exhibit: (1) a resistance to definition and to an account that will not vary from one context to another; yet (2) a propensity to employment in diverse contexts in spite of acknowledged differences in meaning. Both features are necessary ... Even generic expressions may not always be amenable to definition. But for all their vagueness and 'open texture', the characteristic role and utility of general terms demand that they function within a congenial context unless forcibly and appositely removed, as in metaphor.

In fact, the recognition of vagueness in generic usage, threatening as it appears to this initial distinction, cannot but contribute to my general aim. For by undermining the mystique of definition as a search for an underlying common element, it helps reduce the demand for locating a core of meaning common to the varied uses of an analogous term. What *is* common to these diverse yet not unrelated uses seems to lie more on the side of intent. And this is related to the essential difference between generic and analogous usage: the *need* to use certain expressions in widely diverse contexts, coupled with the fact that we do so use them and use them freely. As may be suspected, the need will turn out to be more significant than the fact, though the facts confirm that the need is not esoteric but indigenous. (APL, 23–4)

Burrell recognizes that a properly Wittgensteinian conception of generic expressions must recognize that they might possess the first feature he cites as distinctive of analogous expressions; as the rest of his discussion makes clear, he is thinking in particular of Wittgenstein's notion of family resemblance concepts (whose meaning we explain by citing paradigmatic examples together with a similarity rider). However, he associates this propensity to resist definition with a tendency towards vagueness, which suggests to me that his understanding of the nature of a family resemblance concept has limits.

Wittgenstein introduces the notion of family resemblance by example—the concept of a game. He claims that there is no quality or property that is common to all the various things we call games, and in virtue of which we apply the same term to each one, but rather a complicated network of overlapping and criss-crossing similarities, sometimes very general, sometimes very specific:

> I can think of no better expression to characterize these similarities than 'family resemblances'; for the various resemblances between members of a family: build, features, colour of eyes, gait, temperament, and so on and so forth—overlap and criss-cross in the same way.—And I shall say: 'games' form a family. (PI, 67)

Wittgenstein's moral is radically minimal, even negative. He says that some concepts have a family resemblance structure, not that many, most, or all do, let alone that they must; and he says this purely in order to put in question the assumption that the applicability of any concept is necessarily a matter of the presence of a specific common feature or set of properties, and so that the meaningfulness of a term is a matter of determining the necessary and sufficient conditions for its application.

Bede Rundle has objected even to this minimal reading of Wittgenstein's purposes—that is, to the very idea that any concept might have such a structure. For according to the idea of family resemblance, two items could in principle fall under the same concept and yet have no features whatever in common, without the concept being ambiguous or lacking in unity of meaning; but

> if we had two games which really did have nothing of relevance in common, then we should surely be prepared to say without further ado that the common description could not apply to both univocally . . . if a term behaved as Wittgenstein considers 'game' to behave, then . . . we should simply have to ascribe more than one meaning to that term.[3]

---

[3] *Wittgenstein and Contemporary Philosophy of Language* (Oxford: Blackwell, 1990), pp. 49–50.

Rundle here takes himself to be reminding us of the grammar of our concept of 'equivocity'; any situation in which a word applies to two items that have no common feature is one in which the criterion for the word's meaning being equivocal between the two cases has been satisfied (think of 'bank' as applied to riverbanks and financial institutions). But he fails to distinguish between a case in which two such instances are linked by a chain of overlapping resemblances via intermediate cases, and one in which no such chain is to be found. The latter case might well make the concept of equivocity applicable; but is the same so obviously true of the former?

Take the word 'picture', which denotes amongst other things abstract paintings, representational paintings, and films (i.e. motion pictures). Although abstract paintings and films each have something in common with representational paintings, there seem to be no relevant features common to a Jackson Pollock drip painting and a projected image of Humphrey Bogart; and yet we have no inclination (do we?) to say that the word has one meaning in a conversation about *Casablanca* and another when the talk turns to *Lavender Mist*. To be sure, if someone were to construct such a pattern of use from scratch, we might find it rather puzzling; but if we see it as the result of a process of historical development, the puzzle dissolves. In the case of 'picture', the original focus on representational painting naturally licences an extension of the term's use to photographs (understood as another sort of representation) and thence to motion pictures; and developments in painting also made natural a different extension of the term to include canvasses of a non-representational sort.

In short, Rundle fails to see language in its historical dimension. A purely synchronic perspective makes it almost impossible to understand how a single concept can be forged through a chain of overlapping resemblances; but when it is seen as the outcome of diachronic filiation, as emerging in response to technological and artistic changes in human forms of life and along routes of shared natural reactions, then it becomes intelligible—not predictable in detail, but retrospectively comprehensible. The image of a family resemblance is, after all, perfectly designed to capture the embeddedness of language in time and worldly circumstance, in the complex interplay between nature and culture (as ties of blood are legally or ceremonially bound into those of other families, their intermarriage bequeathing new possibilities of resemblance and difference to their offspring), in our natural history. And of course, such graftings and renewals produce an inherently unpredictable distribution of resemblances; we cannot tell in advance which offspring will resemble which parent, and in which respects.

Wittgenstein thereby questions our assumptions about conceptual unity: his denial that family resemblance concepts must be implicitly or latently equivocal hangs together with denying that, if they were univocal, that unity must be articulable in terms of an algorithmic or *Merkmal* definition. So far, so Burrellian, one might think. But the idea of family resemblance concepts also puts pressure on another assumption—namely, that unitary meaning requires absolute determinacy of sense; as Wittgenstein's imaginary interlocutor puts it, once he appreciates that the overlapping structure of 'game' doesn't have precisely fixed boundaries, '"[I]f the concept 'game' is without boundaries in this way, you don't really know what you mean by a 'game'"' (PI, 70). Against this, Wittgenstein points out that a concept with blurred edges is perfectly usable, and in some contexts more useful than one with rigid boundaries; but he also contests the legitimacy of characterizing a family resemblance concept (as Burrell seems to wish to) as vague or indeterminate at all. For such a characterization is peculiarly absolute or unconditioned—quite as if we can judge a concept to be vague or exact in itself, without any reference to the context and purpose of its employment, as if we have a clear idea of what it might be for a concept to be absolutely precise or determinate:

'Inexact' is really a reproach, and 'exact' is praise. And that is to say that what is inexact attains its goal less perfectly than does what is more exact. So it all depends on what we call 'the goal'. Is it inexact when I don't give our distance from the sun to the nearest metre, or tell a joiner the width of a table to the nearest thousandth of a millimetre? (PI, 88)

To say that 'game' lacks determinacy of sense is thus itself a remark lacking in sense, for it fails to specify the ideal of determinacy being employed, or to relate that ideal to a comprehensible, context-specific goal that the relevant concept with its particular structure prevents us from attaining. Without such a specification, the charge of lacking determinacy or univocity of meaning is not so much misplaced as devoid of substance.

It would therefore be preferable if Burrell did not concede the idea of vagueness to his opponent in this particular dialectical context: it is both unnecessary and potentially deeply misleading. That said, retracting the concession leaves Burrell's underlying argument unaffected, since he emphasizes that analogous uses can be distinguished from generic ones only if both of the criteria he employs to pick out the former are satisfied—not only their resistance to definition, but also their propensity to employment in diverse contexts in spite of acknowledged differences in meaning from context to context. Family resemblance concepts would not satisfy that second criterion (the diversity of accepted instances of games is not such as to lead us to acknowledge differences in meaning— on the contrary). Setting that case aside, however, how helpful would it be to regard other generic or ordinary uses of words as satisfying the second of Burrell's criteria for analogous usage? To what extent is the propensity to employ words in a diversity of contexts a feature of wordhood as such, rather than being a feature of specifically analogous usage?

The reader of Wittgenstein who has made out this case most extensively is Stanley Cavell; its exemplary articulation is in *The Claim of Reason*,[4] in his 'Excursus on Wittgenstein's Vision of Language'. Cavell's primary example of the ways in which we (as he puts it) project our words is that of 'feed'. We learn to 'feed the cat' and to 'feed the lions', and then, when someone talks of feeding the meter or feeding our pride, we understand them; we accept this projection of it. On Cavell's view, tolerating such projections is of the essence of words. We could, of course, have used other words than 'feed' for such a new context, either by projecting another established word or inventing a new one. If, however, we talked of 'putting' money in the meter as we do of putting a dial on the meter, we would lose a way of making certain discriminations (between putting a flow of material into a machine and putting a part made of new material on a machine), we would begin to deprive ourselves of certain of our concepts (could we dispense with talk of feeding our pride and still retain our concept of emotions as capable of growth?), and we would be extending the legitimate range of our alternative word in just the manner we were trying to avoid. If instead we invented a new word, we would lose a way of registering connections between contexts, open up questions about the legitimate projections of

---

[4] Oxford: Oxford University Press, 1979; new edition 1999, hereafter CR.

this new word, and at the limit deprive all words of meaning (since no word employed in only one context would be a word).

Nevertheless, our projections of our words are also deeply controlled. We can, for example, feed a lion, but not by placing a bushel of carrots in its cage; and its failure to eat them would not count as a refusal to do so. Such projections fail because their connection with other words in their normal contexts do not transfer to the new one; one can only refuse something that one might also accept, hence something that one can be offered or invited to accept; and what might count as an offer and an acceptance in the context of a meal is both different from and related to what counts as an offer and acceptance in the context of mating or being guided. These limits show how what Cavell elsewhere calls a word's grammatical schematism determines the respects in which a new context for a word must invite or allow its projection:

I am trying to bring out, and keep in balance, two fundamental facts about human forms of life, and about the concepts formed in those forms: that any form of life and every concept integral to it has an indefinite number of instances and directions of projection; and this variation is not arbitrary. *Both* the 'outer' variance and the 'inner' constancy are necessary if a concept is to accomplish its tasks—of meaning, understanding, communicating etc., and in general, guiding us through the world, and relating thought and action and feeling to the world. (CR, 185)

Despite the binary imagery, Cavell does not in fact believe that a concept's constancy is more internal or integral to its capacity to accomplish its tasks than its variance, or that its essence is determined by conjoining two separable components or elements; rather, its projectibility has an indefinitely variable kind of constancy, or an essentially non-arbitrary kind of variation. Cavell's two fundamental facts are in truth two aspects of a single phenomenon; they do not need to be kept in balance, because to downgrade or occlude one is to distort the other.

This dual-aspect vision is grounded in Cavell's earlier specification of his (and what he takes to be Wittgenstein's) notion of a criterion:

[Wittgensteinian] criteria do not relate a name to an object, but, we might say, various concepts to the concept of that object. Here the test of your possession of a concept . . . would be your ability to use the concept in conjunction with other concepts, your knowledge of which concepts are relevant to the one in question and which are not; your knowledge of how various relevant concepts, used in conjunction with the concepts of different kinds of objects, require different kinds of contexts for their competent employment. (CR, 73)

Knowing what a toothache is, is in part a matter of knowing what counts as having a toothache, what counts as alleviating a toothache, and so on. The grammatical schematism of a word is its power to combine with other words:

the word's potency to assume just those valences, and a sense that in each case there will be a point of application of the word, and that the point will be the same from context to context, or that the point will shift in a recognizable pattern or direction. (CR, 77–8)

Hence when the acceptability or naturalness of a new projection of a given word is in question, our final judgement will turn upon the speaker's capacity to show that and how the new context into which she has projected it either invites or can be seen to allow that projection by inviting or allowing (at least some modified form of) the projection of those other words to which its criteria relate it, and which are accommodated in familiar contexts of the word's use.

Many of Cavell's examples of projections are utterly obvious to us; they show the untroubled reach of our mutual attunements. We accept that placing a bushel of carrots in a lion's cage does not count as 'feeding' him because (amongst other things) we can see nothing that could count as his accepting or refusing to eat it; but we also accept talk of feeding the meter and feeding our pride despite the fact that much of the word's familiar valences either will not carry over or must be modified in order to do so. We understand someone who says that the meter has refused her coins, or that her pride refuses to feed on such gross flattery; the valences of 'refusal' in these contexts differ not only from one another but from their more familiar contexts (in the lion's cage or the fast-food restaurant), but the point of their modified retention—the point of the word's application—is clear. In other cases, the acceptability of the projection is less clear; it isn't obvious how and why we should accommodate ourselves to it, because it isn't clear how the word's valences might be carried over into its new context. Imagine a plank stood on end about the height and width of a human being, tipped and braced back slightly from the vertical, into which are fitted at right angles two pegs to go under the armpits and a saddle peg in the middle—is such a thing a chair? Well, would we be inclined to count the tribesman comfortably arranged on its pegs as sitting on it?

Different questionable projections will elicit different forms of justification and criticism, and reach different kinds of individual and communal resolution. It will not be clear in advance exactly what might be said to justify or to criticize a disputed projection—that will depend on the disputants' knowledge of the new context for the word, their capacity to give explicit articulation to their implicit grasp of the word's criteria, the depth and range of their imaginations, their willingness to accommodate change in exchange for insight, their sense of a given concept's grammatical centre of gravity, and so on. But to know how to speak is to know what kinds of consideration are pertinent to the justification and criticism of a given word's projections; we might see good reason to deny that what the tribesman is doing with his plank is sitting on it, but we thereby acknowledge that determining whether anything might count as sitting on the plank contributes to determining whether that plank counts as a chair. Without that shared grasp of canons of relevance, there would be nothing of the systematic normativity in language use to which Wittgenstein and Cavell are so sensitive, and without which grammatical investigations could have no claim on our attention.

It's worth acknowledging that Wittgensteinians of a very different temperament are also willing to acknowledge the phenomenon on which Cavell focuses. In a recent essay, Peter Hacker has stressed the prevalence of what he calls (in a turn of phrase likely to appeal to a Thomist like McCabe) word-clusters and analogical relations of meaning in natural languages. His preferred example is 'running': he points out that we speak of animals running, taps running, rivers running, paint running, stains running, routes running (from A to B), and of politicians running (for office). For Hacker, these expressions are related by analogy; and the meaning of a given expression within a cluster cannot always be represented as derived by a set operation from another, because the analogies involved are neither regular nor predictable, and there is no way of circumscribing the operative similarity. In fact, Hacker claims that even 'if there is any hidden regularity that an ingenious linguistic theorist might discover, it is just that: a regularity, not a rule that we use to guide us or invoke to explain what a phrase means' (Hacker, WUM: I, 178[5]).

---

[5] *Wittgenstein: Understanding and Meaning*, Parts I and II (Oxford: Blackwell, 2005), hereafter WUM.

Opinions may differ about how pervasive such word-clusters are, and hence how dependent upon analogical relations our use of language may be—although Hacker himself says that 'Wittgenstein stressed the pervasive role of analogy in language' (WUM: I, 177). And some who acknowledge the phenomenon to be ubiquitous—such as Cavell—might resist labelling the phenomenon as a 'word-cluster', since that risks suggesting that each point along the projection carves out a distinct meaning of (or way of meaning) the given word, as opposed to unfolding or articulating its distinct meaning. Nevertheless, Hacker and Cavell have identified a dimension of language use that subverts the idea that the grammar of a word licences certain uses of it and excludes certain other uses, unless and until the rules governing its use are modified (individually or collectively) to determine a new use for it. And in so doing, they have subverted the picture of linguistic normativity as atomic or discontinuous that underlies the all-too-natural sense that if a word is not univocal it must be equivocal. For how would that model apply to Hacker's 'running' or Cavell's 'feeding'? When we go on from talking of a lion running to talk of a river running and then of a route running (from A to B), are we in each case forging a new set of grammatical rules (and so a new language-game) with the word, and thereby changing its meaning at every point of the projection? Or is it rather part of what it is be a word (part of the grammar of the word 'word') that it be capable of bearing up under such unpredictable projections into new contexts, and so part of understanding it that one be willing and able to keep up with its unfolding adventures in the world, and so with the world's unpredictable unfolding of itself?

Perhaps the most striking example of such unpredictable exfoliations of sense that finds acknowledgement in Wittgenstein's work involves what he calls the primary and secondary meanings of words:

Given the two concepts 'fat' and 'lean', would you be inclined to say that Wednesday was fat and Tuesday lean, or the other way round? (I am strongly inclined towards the former.) Now have 'fat' and 'lean' some different meaning here from their usual ones?—They have a different use.—So ought I really to have used different words? Certainly not.—I want to use *these* words (with their familiar meanings) *here*. . . .

Asked 'What do you really mean here by "fat" and "lean"?', I could only explain the meanings in the usual way. I could *not* point them out by using Tuesday and Wednesday as examples.

Here one might speak of a 'primary' and 'secondary' meaning of a word. Only someone for whom the word has the former meaning uses it in the latter . . .

The secondary meaning is not a 'metaphorical' meaning. If I say, 'For me the vowel e is yellow', I do not mean: 'yellow' in a metaphorical meaning—for I could not express what I want to say in any other way than by means of the concept of yellow. (PI: PPF, 274-8)

Once again, opinions may differ about the pervasiveness and the significance of this phenomenon. Some see it as marginal; I have argued elsewhere that it is emblematic of the productive interaction of nature and culture, an exemplary instance of the ways in which the biological and the sociological dimensions of our forms of life inform one another and open human beings to an undefined future.[6] This is because our willingness to accept a secondary use of a word exemplifies the way in which mastery of language-games, which is itself grounded on our possession of pre-linguistic natural reactions, can create a new realm of spontaneous *linguistic* reactions that can in their turn form the basis of new language-games playable by any who share those reactions: call this our second inheritance of language, through which the depth of our first inheritance of it finds expression. However that may be, it is clear that Wittgenstein distinguishes secondary meaning from metaphorical meaning whilst equally sharply denying equivocality of meaning (exactly as McCabe does with relatedness of meaning, and Cavell with projectibility). We could restrict our use of 'bank' to refer to financial institutions, and use some other word to refer to riverbanks, without loss of sense or significance; but Wittgenstein would certainly not say the same of primary and secondary uses of a word.

To conclude: my claim is that, rather than taking univocity of meaning to be a matter of algorithmic precision, and equivocity (understood as a contingent collocation of equally univocal meanings) as its only alternative, Wittgenstein regards what McCabe calls 'relatedness of meaning' as fundamental to our life with language. One might even say that, on this way of interpreting his later writings, relatedness of meaning does not so much presuppose meanings to be related as make those meanings possible. That relatedness may manifest itself in various ways—in the inherent projectibility of words (both individually and collectively), in the internalization of interrelatedness as unity in family resemblance structures, at the limit in the relation he famously emphasizes between

---

[6] Cf. Mulhall, *Inheritance and Originality* (Oxford: Oxford University Press, 2001), pp. 153-82.

primary and secondary meanings (in which secondary meanings would be nothing without their relatedness to primary meanings). But from this perspective, algorithmic univocity and the purely aggregative equivocity that at once opposes it and is shaped by what it opposes appear as limiting or degenerate cases of normal linguistic phenomena. They are not paradigm cases of what meaningfulness amounts to, but rather highly specialized (and so sometimes extremely useful) variations upon the mutual relatedness and projectibility that is the ordinary condition of individual words. In short, our ordinary language-games are what they are by virtue of their openness to other language-games, and to their creative elaboration (both individual and collective) in the face of the unpredictable future of our worldly life with language.

Wittgenstein's vision of language thus has a deep affinity with the Grammatical Thomist conception of analogical uses of words, in that it allows us to view the analogical patterns of usage on which Aquinas focuses as continuous with the more general phenomena of generic or ordinary meaning to which Wittgenstein is sensitive, and thereby to demystify the very idea of such analogous uses by demonstrating their family resemblance to a wide range of other linguistic phenomena. It also reinforces McCabe's minimalist or negative interpretation of Aquinas' invocation of analogous uses, by encouraging us to think of the kind of meaning-relatedness such uses exemplify as internally related to linguistic normality, to generic or ordinary usage. Wittgenstein's broader conception of language would thus support the Grammatical Thomist view that analogous usage is not something for which a particular theoretical foundation or reframing is needed if it is to pass grammatical muster. And it would further help to make sense of the idea that analogous uses of words tap into and expose something essential to the linguistic as such—what one might call the inherent beyondness of words to themselves, their essential non-self-identity.

Nevertheless, continuity is not identity; so emphasizing it does not compel us to deny equally significant discontinuities between the generic and the analogous—that is, to deny that analogous usages have their own distinctive nature or characteristics. But it should certainly discourage us from attempting to find a suitably general, abstract way of distinguishing the analogous from the generic (since any such schematic criteria are bound to leave open lines of continuity between analogous uses and their more generic counterparts). And it should encourage us to think that we might make more progress by making our analysis more concrete—that is, by attending more closely to the particular *kinds* of analogous usage with which the Grammatical Thomists are in fact most deeply concerned. In other words, rather than focusing on what analogous usage as such might be, we should rather be asking what is theologically and philosophically instructive about two particular kinds of analogous expressions: the perfections and the transcendentals. This will be the central concern of Lecture Five.

Lecture Five

Perfections and Transcendentals

Wittgenstein's Vision of Philosophy

I ended Lecture Four by suggesting that, although a Wittgensteinian understanding of wordhood is in fact congenial to the general Grammatical Thomist desire to demystify analogous usage, and indeed to their more specific desire to see in religious forms of analogous usage an insight into the nature of language as such, the discussion was conducted at a level of generality that made it hard to avoid misrepresenting the phenomena under investigation. In this lecture I propose to concentrate instead (more concretely, and I hope more productively) on the specific kinds of analogous expression with which Grammatical Thomists are in fact almost exclusively preoccupied—what are standardly called perfections and transcendentals.

5.1 Perfections, Paradigms, and Projections

David Burrell has emphasized that it is pre-eminently perfection terms—such as good, or wise—whose use when speaking to or of God Aquinas deems not only licit, but more appropriate than when speaking of created beings; at the same time, however, he insists that we cannot know what they mean in that primary or literal application, only that our use of them necessarily fails to represent adequately what God is. 'The reason for this is that we speak of God as we know him, and since we know him from creatures we can only speak of him as they represent him' (ST, 1.13.2).

To describe an individual creature as wise is to attribute to it a property that it might have lacked; but it makes no sense whatever to conceive of God as an entity with attributes (let alone with perfections he might lack). Indeed, because God is outside any genus or category, insofar as our language embodies a subject–predicate/genus–species grammar (or any analogue thereof), no description we might construct can succeed in signifying a trace of divinity. Nevertheless, Burrell's Aquinas claims that we can register our awareness of the necessary failure of signification involved in saying that 'God is wise' by always conjoining any such description with the claim that 'God is wisdom'; and of course vice versa. For we thereby exploit the grammatical distinction between subject and predicate, and between specifying a substance's essence and denoting its accidents, in a way which manifests our understanding that these structural features of intelligible speech presuppose distinctions where none exist, articulation where there can only be simplicity.

But if these linguistic structures necessarily fail to apply to God, why not simply refrain from using either form of expression in such contexts rather than insisting on using both? According to Burrell, what justifies such insistence is the distinctive nature of perfection terms. First, they can function with equal legitimacy in diverse contexts: we can talk of good parents, good cricket shots, good paintings, and good meals, in each context employing the term properly, although what justifies its employment will differ; and we would not regard any given range of such contexts as exhaustive of the term's reach. Second, perfection terms are achievement terms, in that they pick out paradigms in relation to which we measure the degree to which other entities in the relevant context satisfy that standard. But we also characteristically regard the standard itself as open to critical evaluation, and indeed take it to be indicative of someone's satisfying such a standard that they recognize this fact—as when Socrates declares that his wisdom consists in knowing how unwise he actually is, or when we take a parent's awareness of the extent to which she fails to live up to the ideals of parenting as confirming her exemplary status *qua* parent.

In short, perfection terms apply to paradigmatic instances and the standards they embody are in principle subject to further refinement: i.e. they are indefinitely perfectible (without ever reaching a state of perfection), and they are inherently capable of being projected into new contexts. Given Aquinas' orienting scriptural characterization of God as the origin and end of all things, hence not only the Creator of all but their ultimate end or *telos*, it will naturally make more sense to regard perfection terms as pointing us towards God rather than away from Him. Diamond might call this preferring a promissory connection to a promissory disconnection; as Burrell puts it, 'we need not know how to use the term of God to know that it could be so used by someone who did know how [, and indeed that] that use would certainly offer the paradigm for all others' (AGA,[1] 64).

Of course, the idea of realizing a particular paradigm beyond any possibility of criticism, as well as that of a paradigm of all paradigms, in relation to which any and all context-specific paradigms appear absolutely or unconditionally imperfect, together project the concept beyond the conditions of its own intelligible use (which are non-accidentally specific to a given context and so to specific kinds of created thing). But in so projecting it, we can (I think) make sense of the sense that we are thereby bringing the distinctive nature of paradigmatic evaluative terms to their fullest possible expression—call it perfecting the use of perfection terms, by projecting the idea of a language in which their incessantly self-critical projectibility might at once fulfil itself and overcome itself, and thereby (like every other created thing) find peace.

Unlike Aquinas, Wittgenstein gives no particular attention to perfection terms in his later work; but that work as a whole embodies a suggestive conjunction of perfectibility and projectibility. Perfection terms (with their apparently inexhaustible willingness to make a home for themselves in diverse contexts) plainly presuppose projectibility; but if the idea of projectibility as such also involves the idea of perfectibility, and we follow Cavell's Wittgenstein in regarding projectibility as essential to wordhood, then the distinctive analogical employment of perfection terms could be regarded as fulfilling, and so disclosing, something in the nature of language as such.

As we have seen, understanding a word—mastering its grammatical schematism—means grasping its distinctive power to combine with other words, together with the point of applying it. Determining the legitimacy of any new projection will therefore depend on a speaker's capacity to give explicit articulation to her implicit grasp of the relevant criteria, on the depth and range of her imagination, and so on. But such determinations ineradicably involve evaluation—the exercise of right

---

[1] *Aquinas: God and Action* (London: Routledge and Kegan Paul, 1979), hereafter AGA.

judgement from case to case concerning what is lost and what gained by redirecting a word's projective trajectory, and concerning the point of marrying just this word to just this context. As Wittgenstein puts it, 'concepts...are the expression of our interest and direct our interest' (PI, 570); and this means that the projections we find ourselves willing (or unwilling) to accept do not so much give expression to some prior understanding we have of the relevant words as constitute occasions on which we clarify and deepen that understanding. When we judge that the tribe's shaped planks really are a kind of chair, or that pride really is something that can be fed, our understanding of what a chair is and what sitting might be, or of what pride is and what feeding might be, has thereby been refined rather than redefined or merely reiterated. Given sufficiently diverse contexts, each inviting in its own way, might not any language user feel tempted to say that what they have thereby come to understand about their words is how little they hitherto understood them, and how much deeper that understanding might become? In short, the idea of words as inherently projectible naturally engenders the idea of our understanding of them, and so of what we thereby understand, as perfectible.

And this in turn relates the perfectibility of words to a perfectionist conception of the self. For if one cannot make right judgements about projecting words into unforeseeably diverse contexts without reflecting on how well that word in that context would maintain its power to articulate the interests and needs to which it gives expression, then refining our understanding of our words is inseparable from refining our understanding of our needs and interests, and so of ourselves. It is no coincidence that Cavell's work after *The Claim of Reason* has increasingly elaborated upon Wittgenstein's participation in what he calls a dimension of moral thinking in the West—that of Emersonian moral perfectionism.

According to this conception, the structure of the self is analogous to the Grammatical Thomists' conception of the structure of words—inherently self-transcending or self-overcoming, and so non-self-identical. Moral perfectionism understands the soul as on an upward or onward journey that begins when it finds itself lost to the world, say disoriented or unintelligible to itself, recovery from which requires a refusal of its present state in the name of some further, more cultivated or cultured, state. However, each such unattained state of the self is no sooner attained than it projects another, unattained but attainable, state, to the realization of which we might commit ourselves, or whose attractions might be eclipsed by the attained world we already inhabit. Because in that sense no state of the self is final or perfect, in another sense every attained state of the self is (that is, can present itself as, and be inhabited as) perfect—as in need of no further refinement. Hence the primary internal threat to moral perfectionism is that of regarding human individuality as harbouring a specific and realizable state of perfection (even if a different one for each individual), rather than as a continuous process of self-perfecting (selfhood as unending self-improvement or self-overcoming, hence as inherently transitional, always already split or doubled, and so a matter of becoming rather than being).

It would, accordingly, be no more alien to Wittgenstein than to Grammatical Thomists such as Burrell to see an internal relation between a perfectionist vision of words and a perfectionist vision of the self. Not only is each vision analogous to the other; actualizing either vision involves actualizing both. For inherently language-using animals, managing the relation between one's attained and unattained states (call it one's self-relation) must involve managing one's relation to one's words. Indeed, recognizing oneself as currently disoriented with respect to one's words, and committing oneself to overcoming that settled state of unintelligibility to oneself, is exemplary of what moral perfectionism asks of its adherents—a paradigmatic instance of the kinds of struggle and self-overcoming that more broadly pervade our lives with one another. What is at stake in moral perfectionism more generally can be at stake in the way we manage our relation to any of the words we claim to master; in that sense, our relation to our words has an ineliminably ethical dimension.

We now have three reasons for thinking that, although grammatical reminders about perfection terms are not a central topic within it, Wittgenstein's philosophical project as a whole is nevertheless marked by their distinctive nature. First, insofar as Wittgenstein claims that what he does is done in the name of 'philosophy' (however reconceived), he proclaims that it gives expression to the love of wisdom—and both 'wisdom' and 'love' are perfection terms. (If this point strikes you as merely an artefact of anachronistic disciplinary labelling, that would strike me as evidence of the way in which our self-understanding as philosophers can suffer radical impoverishment as well as refinement.) Second, Wittgenstein specifically characterizes his writing as a struggle against the bewitchment of the intellect by means of language: the grammatical ambiguity of this formulation locates language as both the means of our bewitchment and of its overcoming, and thereby relates philosophy's *telos* to that of perfecting our understanding of words. For in identifying specific ways in which our projections of particular words can result in their losing touch with their grammatical schematisms, we deepen our understanding of each schematism, and our understanding of the schema-based projectibility of words as that which makes possible all such losses and recoveries of orientation. And third, the terms characteristic of grammatical investigations as such—the signature concepts through which Wittgenstein works on any specific topic—are analogous to perfection terms, in being analogously and appraisively employed.

Take the concept of a language-game. It proclaims its origin as a conjoined projection of the concepts of 'language' and 'game', thereby effecting a marriage between *the* two concepts that Wittgenstein explicitly declares have a family resemblance structure, and that motivate his discussion of the very idea of such a category. By inheritance, therefore, the concept has a genealogical unity, its apparent synchronic multiplicity graspable only as the result of diachronic filiation in response to specific philosophical interests and concerns encountering specific necessities and opportunities of culture and nature. Its appropriate mode of explanation will accordingly be by reference to a range of examples together with a similarity rider, as Wittgenstein explains early in the *Investigations* when discussing an imaginary use of language in which builders employ four terms to denote four types of building stone when ordering one another to fetch and carry them:

In the practice of the use of [the builders' language in section 2] one party calls out the words, the other acts on them. However, in instruction in the language the following process will occur: the learner *names* the objects; that is, he utters the word when the teacher points at the stone.—Indeed, there will be an even simpler exercise: the pupil repeats the words after the teacher—both of these being speech-like processes.

We can also think of the whole process of using words in [section] (2) as one of those games by means of which children learn their native language. I will call these games *'language-games'* and will sometimes speak of a primitive language as a language-game.

And the processes of naming the stone and of repeating words after someone might also be called language-games. Think of certain uses that are made of words in games like ring-a-ring-a-roses.

I shall also call the whole, consisting of language and the activities into which it is woven, a 'language-game'. (PI, 7)

This explanation simultaneously invokes games through which children learn a language, games they play once possessed of language, and what Wittgenstein calls linguistic wholes (either units of a language or a—perhaps primitive—language taken as a whole). That initial polyvalence already ensures that going on with the concept, judging how to project it into diverse new contexts, will be a matter of exercising right judgement with respect to its grammatical schematism, which means evaluating the philosophical costs and benefits involved in responding to any such invitation.

We might call this a matter of reflecting on how best to maintain the spirit of the clarificatory enterprise in whose service the signature concept was forged, which means grasping the point of that enterprise, and so the purposes of its originator—issues that I can testify reveal themselves over time to have a perfectionist structure. And quite as if declaring the analogous status of the concept, Wittgenstein ends his discussion of method in the *Investigations* by asserting that:

Our clear and simple language-games are not preliminary studies for a future representation of language—as it were, first approximations, ignoring friction and air resistance. Rather, the language-games stand there as *objects of comparison* which, through similarities and dissimilarities, are meant to throw light on features of our language. (PI, 130)

So it is not just that the term 'language-game' is explained by reference to exemplary instances; the particular language-games inhabiting Wittgenstein's text are themselves imaginative and imagined paradigms. Grasping how they are to be applied is a matter of noting dissimilarities as well as similarities, and so a matter of evaluating the point or significance of any given comparison in the context of some given philosophical conversation about a particular confusion.

The final initial exemplification of the term 'language-game' seems to run counter to this—that in which it refers to some relatively self-sufficient unit of a broader language, together with its interwoven activities. But even here, questions will inevitably arise about how to distinguish such a unit from others—questions whose nature and significance return us to the inherently analogous nature of the term, and that explicitly surface in his remarks (late in Part I of the *Investigations*) concerning our concept of understanding:

We speak of understanding a sentence in the sense in which it can be replaced by another which says the same; but also in the sense in which it cannot be replaced by any other...

In the one case, the thought in the sentence is what is common to different sentences; in the other, something that is expressed only by these words in these positions.

Then has 'understanding' two different meanings here?—I would rather say that these kinds of use of 'understanding' make up its meaning, make up my *concept* of understanding.

For I *want* to apply the word 'understanding' to all this. (PI, 531–2)

Once again, relatedness of meaning is at issue: these two kinds of use of the word 'understanding' make up a single meaning, and what ultimately shows this is that we want to apply the same word in both contexts—we are naturally inclined to project the word in this way, and so to relate or unify those contexts. So this discussion of understanding naturally raises a question that too few people realize Wittgenstein (that fanatical identifier of meaning and use) is even willing to take seriously—whether, when, and how far differences in use really amount to differences in meaning.

Why (he asks) are we so confident that the word 'is' is used with two different meanings in 'The rose is red' and 'Two times two is four', despite the fact that we use the same word for both senses?

One would like to say that these two kinds of use don't yield a single meaning; the union under one head, effected by the same word, is an inessential coincidence.

But how can I decide what is an essential, and what an inessential, coincidental, feature of the notation...?

[I]n draughts a king is indicated by putting one piece on top of another. Now won't one say that it's inessential to the game for a king to consist of two pieces?

So I am inclined to distinguish between essential and inessential rules in a game... The game, one would like to say, has not only rules but also a *point* [and] one [sometimes] does not see the point of [a] prescription.

If I understand the character of the game aright, I might say, then this isn't an essential part of it. (Meaning – a physiognomy.) (PI, 561–8)

By implication, the ability to make such judgements about semantic singularity or plurality is an essential feature of mastery of any and all language-games—that is, essential to linguistic understanding as such, and essential to Wittgenstein's philosophical methods for understanding such linguistic understanding. For to grasp the meaning of a word is not simply to know the rules governing its use; it is also a matter of grasping the point or purpose of those rules in any given context, which means understanding the character of the game they constitute, its unifying physiognomy—whether the extended patterns of its use exemplify a single, individual expression or a number of them.

There is a clear connection here with Wittgenstein's discussion of seeing aspects:

The familiar face of a word, the feeling that it has assimilated its meaning into itself, that it is a likeness of its meaning—there could be human beings to whom all this was alien. (They would not have an attachment to their words.)—And how are these feelings manifested among us?—By the way we choose and value words . . .

A *great deal* can be said about a subtle aesthetic difference—that is important.—The first remark may, of course, be: '*This* word fits, *that* doesn't'—or something of the kind. But then all the widespread ramifications effected by each of the words can still be discussed. That first judgement is *not* the end of the matter, for it is the *field* of a word that is decisive. (PI, 294-7)

Wittgenstein's treatment of the word 'understanding' implies that these remarks characterize not just the localized domain of aesthetic judgement (say, poetic uses of language) but something that is integral to, and exercised throughout, our capacity to use words. He is identifying an aesthetic dimension to linguistic understanding as such, and thereby demonstrating that mastery of words is inseparable from the ability to exercise right judgement about the fine details of similarities and differences between uses of words from context to context, an inherently non-algorithmic sensitivity to relations of meaning across the whole field of language use. But the same must then hold true of the linguistic mastery needed to make appropriately illuminating use of the concept of a language-game, through which precisely that understanding of projectibility manifests itself philosophically. Because the grammar of grammatical investigations is in this sense analogous, it too must have an aesthetic as well as an ethical dimension (more precisely, one might say—echoing the *Tractatus*—that in it ethics and aesthetics are one); and the same must accordingly be expected of Wittgenstein's writings in general, if his textual example really is paradigmatic.

'Language-game' is not aberrant amongst Wittgenstein's signature concepts in functioning this way: Diamond's flexible handling of the concept of 'grammar', and Cavell's interpretation of the concept 'form of life' as simultaneously connoting the biological and the cultural (hence emphasizing the animality of the human animal or the diversity of its cultural manifestations according to context) show that at least two others have the same analogous nature.[2] And the suggestion that any one of them is in this respect exemplary of them all is strongly supported by the fact that Wittgenstein's most concentrated discussion of philosophical method in the *Investigations* (sections 89–133) is saturated with the analogical.

In that sequence, he makes a home for the concept of 'essence' ('We, in our investigations, are trying to understand the essence of language' (PI, 92)), as if demonstrating to anyone who grasps its historical significance for philosophy's self-understanding that even this revolutionary context invites the concept. He defines the nature of a philosophical problem by citing one historical example (Augustine's famous expression of bewilderment about time (PI, 89)), from which he draws a range of general morals—thereby treating the example as paradigmatic, say an analogical model, and the application of those morals as a matter of right judgement from case to case. And he elaborates a conception of the end of philosophy which rejects the idea of a definitive completion of the subject (whether once for all, or by the serial application of a general formula), in favour of one according to which each particular philosophical problem can and will be completely dissolved, in accordance with its specific nature and points of origin, without engendering the impossible expectation that no new problem, or new expression of an old problem, could emerge in the future:

A method is now demonstrated by examples, and series of examples can be broken off.—Problems are solved (difficulties eliminated), not a *single* problem. There is not a single philosophical method, though there are indeed methods, different therapies, as it were. (PI, 133)

If we regard this as the end (at once the conclusion and the *telos*) of Wittgenstein's discussion of his methods, then it matters that its beginning (in section 89) is motivated by his preceding discussion of family resemblance concepts. For unity-in-diversity thereby appears as the

[2] S. Cavell, 'Declining Decline', in S. Mulhall (ed.), *The Cavell Reader* (Oxford: Blackwell, 1996).

beginning and the end of all things methodological for this philosopher—which is why that same unity-in-diversity is thematized at the very beginning of the text that both articulates and applies that methodological stance—in Wittgenstein's opening citation from August-ine's *Confessions* and his exemplary response to it.

In order to contest the univocal picture of the essence of human language ('the words in language name objects—sentences are combin-ations of such names') that he finds in Augustine's words, Wittgenstein asks us to think of the following use of language (call this his originary language-game, the book's first object of comparison or analogical model):

I send someone shopping. I give him a slip of paper marked 'five red apples'. He takes the slip to the shopkeeper, who opens the drawer marked apples; then he looks up the word 'red' in a chart and finds a colour sample next to it; then he says the series of elementary number-words—I assume that he knows them by heart—up to the word 'five', and for each number-word he takes an apple of the same colour as the sample out of the drawer.—It is in this and similar ways that one operates with words. (PI, 1)

He immediately thereafter invites us to imagine a language (construct another language-game, explicitly although only retrospectively acknow-ledged as such) for which the description given by Augustine is right, the builders' language-game to which I referred earlier:

The language is meant to serve for communication between a builder A and an assistant B. A is building with building stones: there are blocks, pillars, slabs and beams. B has to pass him the stones and to do so in the order in which A needs them. For this purpose they make use of a language consisting of the words 'block', 'pillar', 'slab', 'beam'. A calls them out; B brings the stone which he has learnt to bring at such-and-such a call.—Conceive of this as a complete primitive language. (PI, 2)

If the shopping trip exemplifies a way of operating with words for which the description given by Augustine is *not* right,[3] in what respect does it resist Augustine's description? Most obviously, the diversity of the kinds of words it puts to work. Although 'apple' and perhaps 'red' are words of

---

[3] I have elsewhere argued that we might equally well take this shopping trip to be anything but ordinary, and that Wittgenstein is alive to both interpretative possibilities: cf. *Inheritance and Originality* (Oxford: Oxford University Press, 2001), pp. 43–52, here-after 'IO'.

the kind that Wittgenstein claims Augustine was primarily thinking of (nouns, proper names, and perhaps the names of actions and properties), 'five' is not; and the contrast here with the builders seems clear, since all of their words are nouns for the same kind of object. Then the proximate moral of Wittgenstein's tale is that philosophers need to recall and display differences—that language-games are astonishingly various, and that this variety is itself subject to variation over time (as new games come into existence and others suffer obsolescence) (PI, 23).

But it is surely equally striking that the three different words used by the list-writer, the shopper, and the shopkeeper interact with one another as smoothly as do the three people involved in this transaction—each word as if made to work in the company of the others. How the shopkeeper responds to the word 'apple' certainly differs from his modes of response to the words 'red' and 'five', but those responses are coordinated: each relates him differently to a single line on the list, to the items inside one particular drawer, and to the contents of a single bag that he finally hands over to the shopper—the five red apples on which all three words have an equal and integrated purchase, and without which this particular purchase could not have been made. To understand the shopping list is to understand that it asks for five red apples, and not five red tomatoes, or five green apples, or one red apple. It therefore involves grasping how each word operates within a more general linguistic field (those of number, colour, and fruit) whose ranges of application connect the words on the list to an indefinite range of contexts in which number words, colour words, and words for fruit might be put to work. The grocer's counting aloud might equally well have accompanied a bird-watcher's observations; his colour chart might have helped pick out the right fabric with which to upholster his sofa; and the label on his apple drawer might equally well have labelled an illustration in a child's alphabet book.

In short, each way of using these words in this context is what it is because it could also be employed elsewhere; their collective capacity to effect an economic transaction at the grocer's is inseparable from their individual ability to effect a widely ramifying range of equally but differently collaborative operations elsewhere (each differently dependent on the availability of other words with which to achieve something in other environments). Their individual significance is thus constituted by their distinctive place in an interlocking, overlapping, and cross-cutting network of forms of human practical activity. Call this Wittgenstein's way of acknowledging the inherent cross-categoricality of words.

By contrast, the builders' 'language' consists of individual words that shun collaboration with each other (even, apparently, that of conjunction), and that conjure up no other obvious contexts of human practical activity into which they might fit, except perhaps other building sites (as long as they require no other kinds of building stone). It is precisely the perfection of their fit with the four kinds of object they name that reduces their capacity to transcend their current context towards a bare minimum, and raises their self-sufficiency towards a vacuous maximum. Such a conjunction of the primitive and the complete risks depriving us of grounds for regarding what we have before us as a language at all— as a depiction of one amongst a variety of related ways in which one operates with words, a situated part of a form of life with language.

This variety and interrelatedness resurfaces when Wittgenstein restates his critique of Augustine's picture:

If we say 'Every word in the language signifies something', we have so far said nothing *whatever*; unless we explain exactly *what* distinction we wish to make . . .

Suppose someone said '*All* tools serve to modify something. So, a hammer modifies the position of a nail, a saw the shape of a board, and so on.'—and what is modified by a rule, a glue-pot and nails?—'Our knowledge of thing's length, the temperature of the glue, and the solidity of a box.'—Would anything be gained by this assimilation of expressions? (PI, 13–14)

Wittgenstein certainly wants us to question whether anything is achieved by assimilating words and tools in the envisaged manner. If we stretch our initial everyday notion of 'modification' so that it applies not only to those tools which we do normally say modify things (such as hammers) but also to tools about which that thought never crosses our mind (such as a glue-pot), we have to jettison more and more of its initial grammatical schematism, to the point at which it becomes an empty form, which can be applied to any and every tool only because its applicability tells us nothing of substance about how any of them actually works. So advanced, the claim that 'all tools modify something' does not even tell us something true about hammers, since it doesn't tell us anything at all.

But Wittgenstein doesn't deny that the concept of 'modification' can— with sufficient ingenuity and commitment—be extended far beyond its original sphere of reference; on the contrary, he illustrates exactly how that might be done. In short, he acknowledges that the term 'modification' is itself inherently modifiable: it can be projected beyond its initial contexts of use in ways that were not already encoded within it, but that are facilitated by our grasp of the point of its uses within that context, with respect to which we can elicit agreement from others.

So we cannot coherently respond to the Augustinian tool-characterizer by flatly denying that the term 'modifier' can be applied to anything outside its initial context of use; that would be to deprive the term of the very modifiability—call it projectibility—that is implicitly at work in the shopping trip tale, and that is fatefully reduced to a minimum in the builders' 'language-game'. Doing so would amount to countering the Augustinian in a way which aligns us with his most fundamental confusion; and it would obscure the fact that what leads us into the distinctively philosophical condition of failing to mean anything by our words just when we take ourselves to be conveying a metaphysical revelation is the very projective capacity without which words simply would not be words. The root of philosophical bewilderment is here located in the nature of language itself, not some essentially accidental misapprehension of it.

But that same perfectibly projective aspect of the nature of words is also our means of recovering orientation. For Wittgenstein clarifies the situation by drawing an analogy between this claim about words and a claim about tools, thereby inviting us to see that the former would be closer to the truth if it made use of the concept invoked in the latter. He implies that the capacity of words to signify is in truth a matter of their being inherently modifiable, essentially open to new contexts of use in ways that illuminate further reaches of significance in both word and context. And, so modified, the concept of modification is not far from the truth about tools either. A hammer's ability to modify the position of a nail is both a misleading claim about its equipmental nature (insofar as it identifies that nature with one specific task, as the builders' language tethers each of its terms to one kind of object), and an illuminating way of conceiving it (insofar as it invites us to consider hammers, and so all tools, as inherently modifiable, adaptable in analogous ways to ranges of equipmental and non-equipmental contexts). In other words, the way to make both claims at once substantial and illuminating is to modify each in the light of the other: it is a matter of reflectively appraising the words under investigation in the manner best suited to their perfectible projectiveness—namely, analogously.

5.2 Transcendentals: Analogical or Univocal?

Earlier, I offered three reasons for looking at Wittgenstein's philosophical procedures through the lens of perfection terms: as expressing a desire for the love of wisdom, as articulating a perfectionist ethico-aesthetic vision, and as doing so by means of signature concepts designed to be employed analogously and appraisively. Wittgenstein's initial diptych of imaginary language-games reiterates those three considerations, whilst adding another to the list, or at least deepening our understanding of those already on it. For in announcing the inherently cross-categorical tendencies of words, and so the ineliminable interrelation of language-games—emphasizing not only their distinctiveness but their modes of hanging together—it implies that failing to allow for that analogical unity amounts to abolishing what makes words words, and so to occluding whatever makes it possible to represent any category of worldly phenomena. In short, it renders salient that which is presupposed by discourse of any category-specific kind—that which transcends categorical limitation altogether.

These are matters with which philosophers have centrally concerned themselves since Plato under the traditional label of 'the transcendentals'—a group canonically including terms such as 'one', 'true', and 'being', with 'good' typically going proxy for a range of related ethico-aesthetic terms ('order', 'simplicity', 'elegance'). These terms intensify or perfect the cross-categorical projectibility of perfection terms by refusing restriction to any given range of categorical contexts (however diverse)—by functioning trans-categorically. Burrell specifies their distinctive role in linguistic mode:

> If ... I want to say something is the case, I need to be able to fix the subject-matter into an object ('unity'). And since the effort may or may not be successful, I should be able to appraise it ('good') [and] to indicate whether or not I am stating what is the case ('true') ... [N]ote that successful reference includes both the ' ... exists' scheme and the 'p is true' scheme, for we refer with expressions having a sense, and we successfully refer in the event such expressions are true. (APL, 224)

Each specific discursive domain will manifest some version of these schemas, because they appear to signify functions of language which are presupposed by anything else one would want to do with it; but each will flesh them out in its own way, and indeed must do so if it is to constitute a distinct, genuinely substantial kind of world-referring discourse.

'Being' (x is a . . .) reflects no answer in particular but simply notes that the *question* 'What is (the nature of) x?' is a question that will not down. To assert that p is true is simply gratuitous unless the context supplies some clues to the method of verification, to the kinds of statement that could count as evidence. And to say of anything that it is *one* (a unity, an individual) suggests little more than the viewpoint from which someone is regarding it and the general character of his intellectual concern about it. (APL, 223)

The transcendentals are thus privileged terms, in that they schematically signify aspects of language that are essential to its functioning no matter what categorical context it inhabits or extends to; they indicate the presence of order in any domain about which we are in a position to make judgements or appraisals, whilst acknowledging the diversity of its specific manifestations, and so the elusiveness of its essence. They will therefore particularly preoccupy anyone interested (as philosophers are) in speaking of language as a whole, and of the relation between language and the world as such; but since speaking of such things will require using words, and since that of which we desire to speak is not something restricted to a specific categorical domain or set of domains, what words could be better suited to such a task than those belonging to the privileged kind with which we are preoccupied?

Reflecting philosophically on the transcendental structure or order of linguistic judgement is itself an exercise of judgement—an appraisal of our practices of appraisal; so we should expect that philosophical reflection on the order of things will itself have a transcendental structure, constituting one more context in which the categories of 'being', 'unity', 'truth', and 'goodness' will be put to use. At the same time, however, the way in which those terms apply in philosophical appraisal can be expected to differ just as much from the way in which they apply in straightforwardly categorical modes of appraisal as their application in any one such domain differs from their application in any other.

Properly self-aware philosophical accounts of the human capacity to word the world will therefore be sensitive to three interrelated aspects of language. First, they must attend to the categorical differences between modes of discourse (their distinctive modes of individuation, methods of verification, protocols of contestation, etc.). One result of attending to these grammatical differences between modes of language directed at different kinds of subject matter will be the disclosure of any trans-categorical structures which hold them together; so such reflection must (second) recognize the unity-in-diversity of such structures—the fact that what is presupposed by any category-specific mode of discourse is itself variously realized according to context (and so cannot be given the same kind of account as that of terms limited to a specific categorical domain, or set of domains). Since analogous terms are best suited to expressing such unified diversity, they thereby become not only the object but also the medium of this reflective enterprise; so its practitioners must (third) be particularly sensitive to what differentiates such second-order reflexive uses of analogous terms from their first-order counterparts.

We have already seen that analogous terms primarily function to articulate the diverse unity of cross-categorical discursive contexts; so they are perfectly qualified for the task of articulating that which all cross-categorical expressions such as themselves presuppose and exploit—the diverse unity of all category-specific modes of discourse. But their amenability to projection into that new reflexive context—just like their primary ability to make themselves at home in diverse categorical contexts—depends upon their capacity to acknowledge and accommodate themselves to its highly distinctive character without falling into equivocality. Philosophers who truly comprehend the kind of reflective accounting in which they are engaged must therefore find a way of using analogous terms that neither simply reiterates nor flatly negates the more familiar forms of analogous usage that they aspire to account for: analogous form and analogous content must here reflect one another in the only way possible—analogously.

Naturally enough, then, any philosopher with the necessary self-understanding will manifest it in ways which, whilst bearing an affinity with the work of her peers, will nonetheless distinguish her from them—partly in her choice of terms to employ analogously in bringing out the significance of the transcendentals for judgement in general and philosophical judgement in particular, and partly in her ways of employing them. On Burrell's account, Plato's and Aristotle's signature concepts are best understood in this way, as are those of Aquinas, and he devotes much time and effort to supporting that interpretation. But in his introductory remarks, he also mentions Heidegger as being matched only by Wittgenstein in the contemporary philosophical scene for leading lives of reflective inquiring [which] testify that philosophy is an activity and that the skills required to do it and displayed in the doing of it seem little affected by time or the passage of time . . .

Heidegger and Wittgenstein have shown that [the] model of [philosophy as] progressive, accumulating knowledge betrays the very genius of philosophy and subverts its peculiar contribution . . .

I find Wittgenstein more often doing what Heidegger says one ought to be doing. Yet Heidegger's sayings can illuminate along the way, and they have quite unexpectedly illuminated me. So I wish to speak my gratitude to him now, though this may well be the final reference. (APL, 3–5)

Since I share this sense of the two philosophers' uncanny intimacy, it may help to clarify my hitherto abstract remarks about the way genuine philosophy marries analogous form with analogous content, and to prepare the way for admitting Wittgenstein to the company of those who understand genuine philosophizing to require this of itself, if I spend a little time substantiating Burrell's intuition that Heidegger belongs with Plato, Aristotle, and Aquinas in this critical respect.

As is well known, Heidegger's guiding question is the question of the meaning of Being; and he quickly emphasizes the range of reference of this key transcendental. His introductory elucidation of the term 'Being' runs as follows:

In the question which we are to work out, *what is asked about* is Being—that which determines entities as entities, that on the basis of which entities are already understood . . . The Being of entities 'is' not itself an entity . . . Being is always the Being of an entity. (BT,[4] 1.25–6; 2.29)

'Being' is not an entity, not an object or a property of an object, but that which determines any and every object as an object. This means determining it as an object of a particular kind or nature (hence necessarily equipped with properties of a particular kind or nature), and as really existing as opposed to not being there; to be a particular kind of thing, that thing must be, and nothing can be without being something in particular (possessed of an underlying or essential nature). Hence, Being is met with always and only as the Being of an entity; but it is necessarily encountered whenever one encounters anything. And Heidegger is emphatic that the various different ways in which entities disclose themselves to us are simultaneously interwoven with one

---

[4] *Being and Time*, trans. J. MacQuarrie and E. Robinson (Oxford: Blackwell, 1962).

another—that they display what he quotes Aristotle calling a unity of analogy, or a categorical interconnectedness.

Heidegger thinks of ontic sciences such as biology, history, and physics as what results from our making an issue of our implicit everyday understanding of a given range of the world we inhabit. We rigorously thematize it with a view to systematically interrogating it, and develop thereby a body of knowledge which may surpass or even subvert our initial understanding, but which is made possible by it and which is no less open to further questioning. In particular, everything we thereby come to know takes for granted certain basic ways in which the ontic science demarcates and structures its own area of study—conceptual and methodological resources which can themselves be thematized and interrogated (when, for example, a philosopher of science inquires into the validity of inductive reasoning). Such inquiries concern the conditions for the possibility of such scientific theorizing, what Heidegger calls the ontological presuppositions of ontic inquiry; and whether one inquires into them as a practitioner of the discipline or as a philosopher, the subject matter could not be within the purview of a purely intra-disciplinary inquiry (which would necessarily presuppose what is here being put in question). It is, in short, the business of philosophy.

The object of investigation here might be called a regional ontology; every region of ontic knowledge presupposes one, and thus invites this kind of questioning. And the results of that questioning themselves provoke further inquiry: given that each ontic region discloses an ontology, the relations between the various regional ontologies inevitably become a matter for philosophical inquiry. For on the one hand, each ontology will differ from others, as each ontic region has its own distinctive nature. But on the other, each region may open up on to cognate regions (as chemistry might shed light on biology, or as Heidegger thinks theology has deformed anthropology, psychology, and biology (BT, 10)), thus revealing that its ontology bears upon those others; and of course each regional ontology is an ontology—each performs the same determinative function with respect to its region (determines the Being of a certain range or domain of beings), even if differently in each case. How, then, is this synthesis—this plaiting or interweaving—of categorical diversity and categorical unity to be understood? What is it for beings to be? This is the question of the meaning of Being—what Heidegger calls the enterprise of fundamental ontology.

Heidegger does not and could not think of this enterprise as relating to some domain that is essentially distinct from (say, foundational in relation to) regional ontological inquiry—as if Being as such had a domain of its own in addition to the domains of regional ontology, as if we could directly contemplate Being as opposed to one of its regions. On the contrary, since Being is always the Being of some entity or other, then the question of fundamental ontology must always take regional ontologies and their interrelations as its concern; and anyone who pursues a given regional ontological inquiry without reflecting upon how, if at all, its deliverances and presuppositions relate to those of other such inquiries is simply failing to pursue that inquiry in a properly rigorous manner. Fundamental ontology is regional ontology radicalized, or fully realized; it is not an alternative or supplement to regional ontological inquiry, but a manner of relating oneself to it.

The relevant relation is one which acknowledges (as opposed to either repressing or prematurely fixing) the inherently and multiply situated or contextual nature of regional ontological inquiry. This means attending to the way in which it relates to other regional ontological inquiries (or might do so otherwise, or utterly fails to do so), which involves acknowledging the way in which the ontic science from which it arises relates to other ontic sciences (or might so relate or fails to), which in turn involves acknowledging the way in which the aspect of our pre-theoretical understanding of things from which that science arises relates to other aspects of that understanding (or fails to). Every one of these nodes or elements—be it a branch of philosophy, a means of acquiring knowledge, or a mode of practical activity—is what it is by virtue of its actual and possible relations to all of the others; so a proper grasp of any requires acknowledging that relatedness as an undismissable issue, something about which questions can always be posed and inquiries pursued.

Call this Heidegger's context principle. Its implications are widely ramifying, but for present purposes, what is most pertinent is that it embodies a Burrellian perception of the analogical unity of categorically distinct domains of knowledge and sense, and presents an acknowledgement of that internally related diversity as philosophy's most fundamental business. And to complete the Burrellian picture, that basic perception forces Heidegger to forge a distinct set of terms by means of which to bring to the forefront of our attention that which typically conditions and makes possible our everyday comprehending attentiveness to objects of diverse kinds, and indeed our capacity to reflect comprehendingly on the wonderful fact of that comprehension. Those terms—Heidegger's signature concepts—are patently analogical in their significance and modes of application.

Take his key term for the distinctively human mode of being—*Dasein*, or 'Being-there'. Because human beings appear capable of grasping any and every entity they encounter in its Being, Heidegger hopes that grasping what underlies and makes possible that open-ended access to every ontological region will provide a lens through which he might achieve a perspicuous surview of the whole, analogically structured ontological field that this particular being inhabits and comprehends. Hence he begins by defining *Dasein* as the Being of the being who inquires or asks questions: *Dasein* comprehends entities, and interrogates that comprehension with a view to improving it, given the inescapable fact that its understanding is always conditioned, hence always limited and so vulnerable to elaboration, criticism, and refinement.

But since we are here applying that understanding to our own capacity to understand, it must have the same character and enabling conditions as its object. Accordingly, as Heidegger unfolds the immediate implications of that minimal, introductory characterization, it takes him into new contexts and circumstances whose willingness to accommodate the projection of *Dasein* also reveals new ranges of meaning within it, which licence further such projections. So as we follow its progress from context to context, the term is unceasingly reformulated or recharacterized: we discover that *Dasein* is 'Being-in-the-world', 'Being-with', 'Being-anxious', 'Being-care', 'Being-towards-death', 'Being-guilty', and so on (and of course, each new formulation—as its hyphenation declares—embodies its own inner complexities, each element of which is itself open to further unfolding projection). This terminological chain is neither a reiteration of the significance of the original term nor a repeated substitution of new terms for their predecessors—neither univocal nor equivocal. To understand it, we must understand that its trajectory tracks the same word or concept differently inflected by its marriage with further contexts, engendering thereby a deeper or more refined understanding of its initial significance. In other words, it exhibits exactly the unity of meaning in a diversity of contexts that signals analogical usage.

Heidegger's hermeneutic conception of human understanding presents all human discourse as subject to versions of this projectible

perfectibility. But specifically philosophical discourse aspires perspicuously to survey the necessarily self-concealing enabling conditions of
such understanding; so it must expect to employ a more purified or
intensified version of such analogical terminology, one which is specifically designed for ontological and ultimately trans-categorical or transcendental purposes (as the recurrence of the particle 'Being' in the
unfolding of the projection of *Dasein* declares). Heidegger's word for
this reflective and reflexive inflection of analogical usage is 'formal
indication'.

A formally indicative term provisionally indicates an aspect of a
broader whole whose fuller significance unfolds as it (together with its
internally related fellows) is projected further into the various diverse
contexts and regions that the initial phenomenal data (and corresponding introductory explanations) disclose and point us towards; and if
successfully conducted, the improved understanding of the subject matter that results may necessitate their radical reformulation and reoriented
projection. 'Being-in-the-world', for example, is an analogically shaped
formal indication within a broader semantic field. Individually, it aspires
provisionally to disclose the diverse unity of human Being; but its initial
introduction, and its subsequent elaborations and projections, are motivated by an interest in the basic human capacity to grasp beings in their
Being, which is itself informed by an interest in the question of Being.
Unless our grasp of its employment is continuously informed by a
sensitivity to its ramifying relations with a range of related formally
indicative concepts, and an inwardness with the fundamental purpose
behind its introduction and elaboration, we will simply miss the spirit in
and through which Heidegger puts these analogical coinages to use—
namely, in order to understand what Ancient Greek thinkers would have
called the transcendental structures of objecthood, truth, and Being.

Given the nature of Heidegger's orienting question, and his explicit
indebtedness to his predecessors, it may seem fairly transparent that he
too is concerned with that which concerned Plato, Aristotle, and Aquinas. But is it really credible to regard Wittgenstein's later work as
manifesting such an affinity—to view his meta-linguistic concepts as
designed to bring the transcendentals into particular focus? It's perhaps
worth recalling that the passage on the analogous unity of our concept of
understanding that I cited earlier (from PI, section 561) exemplifies the
issue by asking why we regard the concept of 'being' as unitary despite

WITTGENSTEIN'S VISION OF PHILOSOPHY 103

the apparent diversity of its uses (as copula, as sign of identity, and so on). But of course, that could be a purely accidental reference to the canonical transcendental: so I will conclude this lecture by suggesting that the first hundred or so sections of the *Investigations* (from its opening comparison of the shopping trip and the builders to its concluding ascent to methodological matters) can be read as a sustained critical appraisal of two very different ways of conceiving of the canonically transcendental terms 'being', 'truth', and 'unity': one which envisions them as essentially univocal, the other as intrinsically analogous.

The univocal model finds a variety of expressions, at once engendered by and echoing the core Augustinian idea that all wordings of the world are essentially representations or depictions of it: but its univocality is manifest not simply in its assumption that language is essentially univocal, but also in the univocality of the philosophical language that aspires to capture that singular essence. This dual-aspect monotony is present throughout: in the opening claim that all words are names and all sentences are combinations of names; in the assumption that 'Slab!' (as used in the builders' language-game) must be either a word or a sentence (presumably because that meta-linguistic, trans-categorical distinction is unambiguous, exhaustive, and universally applicable); in the Fregean idea that the distinction between entertaining and asserting a sentence is reflected in the internal structure of the asserted sentence—as if all formal facts about a language must be so embodied (presumably because 'formal' is univocally applied to the forms of speech); in the idea that rules always function in the same way in games (PI, 54); and in the idea that the analysis of a sentence is, if right at all, context-invariant (PI, 61)—a claim which blatantly assumes that philosophical analyses of sentences are as univocal in essence as the sentences analysed. All this before the interlocutor's sustained resistance to the idea of family resemblance concepts, and his deep attachment to determinacy of sense—the critical evaluation of which precipitates Wittgenstein's central discussion of method.

This dialectical thread episodically finds more material expression, as when we encounter the idea that attending to the colour of a sample is always a matter of doing the same thing, and a different thing to attending to the shape; or the idea that reality consists of combinations of absolutely simple elements, and so that our trans-categorical notions of simplicity and multiplicity have context-invariant content, whilst

Being itself is rendered inarticulable. But the overall spirit or thrust of the univocal account is itself invariant, and all-too-easily articulated. There is a single or singular essence of language, and so of our ability to think and speak about how things are in reality, and so of the reality of which we speak and think. This means that the transcendental presuppositions of that ability are themselves essentially univocal or algorithmic (so that thought, speech, and reality remain what they are regardless of context or category); and this in turn means that the language in which we give reflective expression to those presuppositions can and must itself be essentially univocal. Its signature concepts will lack any sensitivity either to the specific category of linguistic or material entity to which they apply, or to the specific kind of work they themselves are doing.

But this univocal model of being, unity, and truth is systematically opposed by an analogous one. For Wittgenstein persistently invites his fixated interlocutor(s) to consider the countless different, context-specific kinds of use of all the things we call 'signs', 'words', and 'sentences' (PI, 23); the different kinds of speech act we call 'descriptions' (PI, 24); the variety of roles that rules might have in games (PI, 31, 83); the context-specific variety of ways in which one might point to the colour of something (PI, 33); the very different kinds of word that we call 'names' (PI, 38) and the very different ways in which even canonically proper names such as 'Moses' are employed and explained (PI, 79); the context-relativity of 'simplicity' and 'compositeness' (PI, 47–60); the centrality and diversity of our reliance upon samples, which we might equally well call exemplars (PI, 50), and our freedom to determine whether or not to categorize them as 'tools of the language' (PI, 16); and so on. These terms are all-but-explicitly presented as analogously trans-categorical: they repeatedly recur in highly diverse contexts, in which what will constitute their correct application must be made out differently, but without any implication of equivocality. And when this counter-univocal or anti-algorithmic thread is woven into the discussion of family resemblance concepts, Wittgenstein's point in so doing is not to present the idea of family resemblance as an alternative univocal schema for the transcendental 'concepthood', but rather to show that family resemblance is simply one of a variety of analogously related conceptual forms—call it an analogical model of the unity-in-diversity that is characteristic of our use of the trans-categorical term 'concept', and its reflective relatives.

I am, accordingly, willing to conclude that Wittgenstein merits a place in Burrell's tradition of genuinely self-aware proponents of philosophical reflection. Even so, one might think that my reading of the initial sections of the *Investigations* brings him rather closer to Plato and Aristotle than it does to Aquinas, in that, whereas Burrell presents Aquinas as a thinker whose theology makes manifest his reflective or philosophical understanding of transcendentals as analogous, I present Wittgenstein as doing something analogous in a decisively non-theological context. And yet: can it really be of no significance that the dialectical struggle between univocal and analogous conceptions of trans-categorical terms in the *Investigations* begins with a citation from a Christian saint's autobiography and culminates in a discussion of how we use the name 'Moses' (PI, 79)—the proper name of the man who led the Israelites out of captivity, through the wilderness, to within sight of the Promised Land in which he himself would never live? Does this count as a theological context? What exactly is the relation between philosophy and theology as Grammatical Thomism understands it, and as Wittgenstein (on my reading of him) understands it? This will be the focus of Lecture Six.

Lecture Six

Authority and Revelation
Philosophy and Theology

In Lecture Five, I suggested that the Grammatical Thomists' account of why Aquinas gave theological centrality to perfections and transcendentals casts a great deal of light on otherwise obscure aspects of Wittgenstein's conception of philosophy, and thereby reinforces (rather than subverts) their claim to be inheriting the spirit of Wittgensteinian philosophy in their reading of St Thomas.

The key idea is to see transcendental terms as a kind of transcending or perfecting of cross-categorical perfection terms, which are themselves a kind of perfecting of the projectibility of terms as such. Projectibility and perfectibility are internally related, in that, insofar as our comprehension of any word was subject to endless deepening (or its reverse), this perfectibility was equally pertinent to the meaning of the words understood and to the significance of their user's needs, interests, and desires—hence to their understanding of themselves. This means that our understanding of our words and ourselves is inherently subject to a mode of appraisal that is at once ethical and aesthetic, and not restricted to some specific domain of our life with language. This is what I (following Cavell) have been calling moral perfectionism.

If transcendental terms are seen as perfecting perfection terms—that is, as the intra-mundane epitome of the cross-categorical—then they too are internally related both to perfections and to the projectibility of words, and so should epitomize the ethico-aesthetic dimension of language and linguistic understanding as a whole. Insofar as they articulate the presuppositions of any category of discourse whatever, their schemata emblematize the unity-in-diversity of language as such (the way in which each discursive domain puts different flesh on analogous grammatical bones, simultaneously making manifest their difference from and their affinity with other discursive domains); and insofar as those schemas are a presupposition of comprehending reality, then they also articulate the reality we comprehend—its diverse unity as an interrelated field of distinct kinds of entity.

In that sense, properly to appreciate the role of the transcendentals is to appreciate reality's invitation to us to consider it as a finite whole—so that properly grasping each of its domains requires reflectively determining its relations to others (however analogical those relations may be), just as Kant thinks of an artwork as setting us the task of reflectively grasping how each of its elements contributes to the whole.[1] This is the perspective on reality that the Wittgenstein of the *Tractatus* characterized as intrinsically ethico-aesthetic; and since the core business of philosophy is to understand that which the transcendentals articulate (to understand, in both the particular and the general case, how speech, thought, and reality relate to one another), it follows that philosophy itself aspires to just that ethico-aesthetic perspective.

But there is an important disanalogy between Wittgenstein's way of demonstrating awareness and mastery of the transcendentals and Aquinas' way of doing so, as there is between Aquinas' and Wittgenstein's ways of acknowledging the perfections. For as I emphasized in Lecture Five, Aquinas shows his understanding of perfections by the way in which he projects them into a specifically theological context. By saying that they can more legitimately be applied to God's nature than to any created thing, but only if they are simultaneously applied in adjectival and substantive modes ('God is wise' if and only if 'God is wisdom'), a pattern of usage that he admits is nonsensical, he constructs a theological acknowledgement of God's transcendence that displays his philosophical appreciation of the grammar of perfection terms (their status as paradigm-based cross-categorical appraisals). And insofar as the grammar of perfection terms itself presupposes the trans-categorical status of distinctions such as subject and predicate, essence and existence, copula and identity, there is reason to suspect that Aquinas is equally appreciative of the significance of the canonical transcendentals. For these, too,

---

[1] Kant, *Critique of the Power of Judgement*, trans P. Guyer and E. Matthews (Cambridge: Cambridge University Press, 2001), part 1.

Burrell's Aquinas regards as legitimately applicable to God, but only by virtue of modes of projection that categorically refuse any assignments of sense, and thereby display Aquinas' appreciation of what must be presupposed if sense is to be made.

Take Aquinas' notorious claim that 'to be God is to be "to-be"'. As we saw in Lecture One, Kenny and Rundle both object to this formulation because it blatantly flouts the fundamental grammatical distinction between essence and existence; but that, for Burrell, is precisely its point. 'The form of the assertion fractures a normal form for substantive predication: *to be x is to be y*' (APL, 238); and it does so precisely in order to show that God cannot be spoken of in substance/accident terms, to make it manifest that even the most apparently fundamental transcategorical structures of speech and thought have no application to God. Diamond might say that Aquinas thereby forges a promissory connection between God's transcendent simplicity and the denial of a distinction between his essence and his existence. She might also say that such a strategy achieves the philosophical illumination sought by traditional readings of the *Tractatus*, without committing its proponent to a notion of substantial nonsense. For Burrell's Aquinas displays his grasp of the transcendental formal presuppositions of sense not by constructing propositions that he incoherently conceives as combining individually intelligible ingredients in a logically impermissible way, but by refusing to accept that these words, put together in knowing violation of their everyday patterns of use, should be assigned any (individual or collective) sense.

On Burrell's account, only someone philosophically adept could provide a theology such as Aquinas': only someone who has properly understood the analogous nature and the philosophical privileges of the perfections and the transcendentals could misuse them in such a way as to manifest an understanding of their role in human appraisals of reality and of God's transcendence of both. But that shows only that good theology presupposes good philosophy; it doesn't show that good philosophy can only be done by doing good theology. And if Wittgenstein, like Plato and Aristotle, is rightly understood in the terms I have been developing here, doesn't that demonstrate that there are various ways in which philosophy can achieve genuinely self-aware insight without involving itself with theology?

6.1 Drawing the Circle to End All Circles

How do things look from the perspective of theology—and specifically, of Burrell's Aquinas? First, insofar as Aquinas' theology exploits the analogous nature of perfections and transcendentals, it deprives philosophy of any *a priori* grounds for prohibiting it. If it is of the essence of words to be projectible, and of perfection terms and transcendental terms to be open to indefinite ranges of new contexts in which they might find legitimate habitation without succumbing to equivocity, then it can never be legitimate to dismiss any attempts to project perfections and transcendentals into theological contexts as *necessarily* abusive of their meaning. If those projections are to be rejected, one must ground that conclusion case by case—by arguing that the relevant context does not in fact justify that projection.

Second, such philosophical contestations must be appropriately self-aware. In particular, they must be sensitive to the fact that perfections and transcendentals are deeply woven into *philosophy*. Perfections define its proper name and *telos*; its founding figure exemplifies a willingness to interpret his own wisdom as consisting in his knowledge of the extent to which he lacked it; and philosophy's identity as a specific contributor to the intellectual economy of our form of life depends on the legitimacy of the impulse to attend to the trans-categorical features of language, thought, and reality, and so on a particularly robust exploitation of language's inherent tendency towards cross-categorical projections. Indeed, philosophy's sheer existence is a projection of the inherently human enterprise of appraising reality from its originating category-specific contexts (the intellectual responsibility of physics, history, psychology, and so on) into one in which we appraise the presuppositions which distinguish each category whilst allowing it to have a bearing upon the others; so philosophy's own claim to respect depends upon the very processes of analogous concept-construction upon which Aquinas' theology stakes its corresponding claim. If the step from category-specific judgement to the cross- and the trans-categorical is legitimate, however peculiarly orthogonal or analogous it may be, then what exactly is illegitimate about the equally peculiar analogous step from the trans-categorical to the theological?

Since the theologians I'm considering make a point of emphasizing that their projections deprive the projected words of sense, then the obvious basis for a Wittgensteinian philosophical critique is deprived of any dialectical force. Indeed, the theologian's desire to cleave to those projections despite their senselessness ought rather to make any Wittgensteinian philosopher wonder whether nonsense can serve human purposes, and if so in what ways. And the Grammatical Thomist might respond to that question by claiming that the step from the transcategorical to the theological is not only entirely consistent with the prior step that brings philosophy into being; it is in fact the fulfilment of that impulse, and so of the enterprise of reflective appraisal that it engendered. In perfectionist terms: theology is the self-overcoming of philosophy, the next or further, unattained but attainable state of itself. It is a condition within which everything that philosophy has painstakingly learnt and relearnt about the trans-categorical (and everything it presupposes) is at once fully acknowledged and decisively transcended, by the construction of a 'perspective' in relation to which any philosophical acknowledgement of these matters will appear essentially limited or imperfect.

Aquinas' Five Ways might be read as encapsulating just this line of thought. In Lecture Three, I presented them in ontological mode, as displaying the structural multiplicities internal to thinghood, to existence as one entity possessed of a nature and part of a system of nature; but one might equally well present them as epistemological (that is, as making manifest the conditions for the possibility of a rational accounting of the system of nature) or—à la Burrell—as semantic (showing the conditions for the possibility of representing reality, or wording the world). So understood, they articulate everything that philosophy can tell us about ourselves as rational animals, participants in nature possessed of the ability and the desire to understand every kind of thing that participates in nature, including ourselves and our understanding. So there is nothing philosophy can tell such a theology—nothing belonging to philosophy's distinctive mode of reflective appraisal that such theology does not already know.

But does the right kind of theology have something to tell philosophy—something it knows that the other does not, and so of which it might inform its predecessor? In one sense, 'No': for the Grammatical Thomist view is that the linguistic constructions to which theology is driven do not constitute an intelligible language. When we say that God is wise and God is wisdom, or that to be God is to be to-be, we do not know what we mean by these statements; they are, in Diamond's terms, promissory grammatical connections in a language that we do not know how to use. In that sense, the perspective that theology constructs and holds open is a 'perspective': the linguistic circle that it draws around the distinctive discursive domain of philosophy (and so around all the category-specific domains from which philosophical reflection constitutes itself) is not so much one more discursive domain as the mere or pure promise of one.

On the one hand, this means that theology's way of outstripping philosophy is not dependent on any single articulated disposition of philosophy's domain. Aquinas's Five Ways are inevitably beholden to the best available philosophical understanding of his time (Aristotle's). But since they work by extending the necessarily analogous and apparently pervasive schemas of appraisive judgement as such, the same theological project—the same projection of theology beyond philosophy's best understanding of the ontology, epistemology, and semantics of the human relation to reality—will be feasible whatever revisions and reformulations that best understanding is subject to over time (whether because of changes in category-specific modes of understanding, or changes in philosophy's best understanding of them).

On the other hand, this confidence in theology's ability to reshape itself to whatever shapes philosophical reflection takes on, rests on the fact that theology does not, strictly speaking, have a shape of its own. For its distinctive domain of discourse is not in truth one more domain of discourse, not even one as unusual in its nature as that of philosophy. Its grammar is (or rather necessarily includes) a 'grammar', one that we construct and cleave to precisely because it resists any assignments of sense and so articulates a 'language' that we cannot speak. It therefore does not delineate an intellectual location—one further dispensation of the logos that might be aligned with philosophy's own, a place that philosophy might occupy or inhabit, an unattained but attainable version of itself. Rather, theology points us beyond any conceivable further state of philosophy, to a 'perspective' for which the very idea of further perfecting is ruled out in advance (through what Diamond might call a promissory grammatical disconnection), whilst fully acknowledging that this does lethal violence to the grammar of perfectionist self-overcoming (for which it is true by definition that around every circle, another can be drawn).

In short, theology's perfectionist relation to philosophy is as analogical as philosophy's relation to category-specific disciplines; and that is why the sheer existence of theology—the fact that there is something called 'theology' rather than nothing—discloses an ineliminable but unappeasable aspiration of philosophy, and testifies to its fulfilment. For insofar as philosophy inquires into the human capacity for comprehending reality, which means appraising both the distinctiveness and the unity of our various particular ways of appraising any particular domain of reality, it amounts to a purified or intensified exemplar of this aspect of the human way of being—a mode of understanding whose object or *telos* is any and all modes of understanding, hence a finite totality of which it is itself a part. But philosophical inquiry must itself be questionable—because it is no less subject to condition and limitation than any other exercise of this capacity, and because anything it establishes constitutes a new addition to its subject matter that might in principle outrun that established understanding of it; hence, it is destined to fail to fulfil its own defining aspiration. In the end, then, the sheer existence of philosophy as a mode of human appraisive judgement reveals that human beings aspire by their very nature to a completeness of understanding that they cannot realize. Philosophy constitutes the place at which finite human understanding endlessly attempts, and as endlessly fails, to take itself in as a whole; and it thereby reveals that it is internal to the nature of finite beings to be subject to the mysterious, unsatisfiable desire to transcend their own finitude.

In taking the analogous perfectionist trajectory of philosophy beyond itself, theology is at once informed by that desire and brings it to full reflective self-awareness. By projecting a perspective from which not only every articulation of human judgement but its basic articulatedness is dispensed with, and explicitly presenting their transcendence as entailing the transcendence of intelligibility, it acknowledges the actual conditions and essential conditionedness of the human understanding of reality in such a way as to testify to our deep dissatisfaction with what we cannot deny is essential to our nature. For by refusing to assign sense to the promissory connections of a 'language' that would transcend any such conditions, theology declares that any conceivable grasp we might attain on reality (and so any reality we can conceive of) could never fully satisfy our most fundamental desire as rational animals. Otherwise put, it declares that if our *telos* and our heart's desire were, *per impossibile*, ever to be realized, then it could only happen outwith anything we could recognize as the horizon of the real, and as the effect of something given to us, not something we can bring about. But by constructing and cleaving to that 'language', it also testifies that there *is* such an elsewhere, that there will be such a gift. In short, theology discloses philosophy's perennial aspiration to a God's eye view as both essential to its nature and essentially beyond its own grasp—not exactly because there is no such perspective, but rather because that perspective is and can only be a 'perspective', hence belongs to God alone, and so is realizable only as and through faith.

Accordingly, whilst Grammatical Thomist theology does not claim to know anything of which it is in a position to inform philosophy, it nevertheless has something to tell it. The analogous model that has been guiding my presentation of theology throughout these lectures is that of solving riddle questions. And this underlines the way in which (like mathematicians attempting to construct a proof with which to tie a conjecture into their existing proof systems) theology extrapolates analogously from established grammatical patterns, thereby disclosing and extending the array of human interests, needs, and impulses that produced them. But if these extensions are analogous to solving riddles, they must be responses to something that invites or rather requires a solution—that is, to forms of words that we encounter as *posing* a riddle, hence as at once enigmatic and magnetic (especially to anyone with a properly self-aware grasp of philosophy's achievements, nature, and importance). Theology must then be in the possession of phrases and formulations that it is compelled to regard as the perfect fit or ultimate *telos* for the human impulses for which perfections and transcendentals are the expressive vehicle; they are fixed points or nodes in a logical space that is not only not-yet-articulated, but beyond any conceivable further imaginative extensions of thought and desire. They are thus worthy of the utmost attention despite our knowing in advance that we will dismiss any conceivable assignment of sense to them precisely on the grounds that it would make them usable by us. So they must have absolute authority for us, the kind of authority that is possessed only by that which they impossibly aspire to refer: God Himself. This is the authority of revelation.

Burrell's reading of Aquinas on the transcendentals here converges with Diamond's reading of Anselm. For Burrell emphasizes that infinitive forms of 'to be' standardly register the obtaining of a given language—not any grammatical connection within it (where essence finds expression), and not any truth-apt conjunction of subject and predicate constructible from it (since existence is not a predicate), but rather the 'fact' that there is something corresponding to the concepts comprising that language. Against this background, Aquinas' claim makes the following point: 'when we utter "to be God is to be to-be" we are saying that God *is* what it is for God-language to obtain' (AGA, 49). If God's essence ever did find expression in the grammar of a language, and God's essence and his existence are one, then for there to be such a language just *is* for there to be something to which that language applies.

As Diamond would put it, God is something whose actuality is a condition for the possibility of conceiving it; he is that without which it is inconceivable that we could possess a language appropriate to him. He is at once the source and the intended object of any language capable of grasping him, and he could be the latter only because he is the former; he is the origin and end of any genuine discourse about divinity. To know how to use such a genuinely substantial religious language, we would (impossibly) have to know God face to face; here and now, we know only that certain words apply rightly to him without knowing how they do (we see him through a glass darkly). But even this is possible only on the basis of his revealed authority, which means on the basis of words authorized by him—the words of the prophets, the apostles, and God Incarnate.

6.2 The Ethics and Theology of Testimony

This, then, is what theology has to tell philosophy; but the relevant speech act is not so much that of assertion (apt for the communication of impersonally accessible information) as that of testimony. It is a willingness to testify that the words one proclaims (whether given directly or appropriated from another, perhaps through the traditions of a church) are God's revelation of himself, that others can and should take our word for it that these words are absolutely not ours but his, hence not to be altered or reformulated or outstripped, but also essentially beyond our comprehension, let alone our mastery. This takes the ordinary grammar of testimony to its analogous limits, for it exposes the one giving testimony to an absolute burden of responsibility. It means presenting oneself not just as someone whose word can be relied upon with respect to some item of knowledge, but as a bearer of divine revelation, which involves subjecting each person to whom one testifies to a correspondingly absolute burden of responsibility—that of deciding whether or not to accept that testimony as revelatory of the divine, hence as posing a riddle in which absolutely everything is at stake. Such speech acts isolate the testifier and the one to whom testimony is given to the fullest possible extent: for insofar as the words themselves resist understanding, they intensify the significance of one's appraisal of the one from whom they were received, call it the authority of their source. This is what Kierkegaard has in mind when he characterizes expressions of faith as bringing the subjective dimension of truth to an absolute maximum.[2]

Nevertheless, the very idea of a connection between authority and revelation is not so much an invention of faith and theology as an analogous extension of something embedded in ethical thought. In *A Common Humanity*, Rai Gaita tells a story about his experiences working in a psychiatric hospital.[3] The patients there were judged to be incurable, and appeared to have lost everything which gives meaning to a human life; they rarely had visitors and were often treated brutishly by the staff. Some psychiatrists were different: they worked devotedly to improve their patients' conditions, and spoke resolutely of their inalienable dignity; and Gaita admired them enormously for it. Then:

One day a nun came to the ward. In her middle years, only her vivacity made an impression on me until she talked to the patients. Then everything in her demeanour towards them—the way she spoke to them, her facial expressions, the inflexions of her body—contrasted with and showed up the behaviour of those noble psychiatrists. She showed that they were, despite their best efforts, condescending, as I too had been. She thereby revealed that even such patients were, as the psychiatrists and I had sincerely and generously professed, the equals of those who wanted to help them; but she also revealed that in our hearts we did not believe this . . .

I admired the psychiatrists for their many virtues—for their wisdom, their compassion, their courage, their capacity for self-sacrificing hard work and sometimes for more besides. In the nun's case, her behaviour was striking not for the virtues it expressed, or even for the good it achieved, but for its power to reveal the full humanity of those whose affliction had made their humanity invisible. Love is the name we give to such behaviour . . .

---

[2] Cf. his *Concluding Unscientific Postscript*, ed. and trans H.V. Hong and E.H. Hong (Princeton, NJ: Princeton University Press, 1992).

[3] (Routledge: London, 2000), hereafter 'CH'.

[A]s someone who was witness to the nun's love and is claimed in fidelity to it, I have no understanding of what it revealed independently of the quality of her love . . . For me, the purity of the love proved the reality of what it revealed. I have to say 'for me', because one must speak personally about such matters. That after all is the nature of witness. (CH, 18–22)

There is plainly a perfectionist structure to this narrative. One, genuinely attractive moral stance is suddenly disclosed as profoundly limited by another such stance that neighbours it, previously unimagined but now undeniably attainable because beyond all question attained by another. This disclosure also discloses the extent to which Gaita's previous grasp of a range of perfection terms—goodness, love, life—was shallow and impoverished; it induces the signature Socratic realization that he had hitherto understood so little of what those terms might mean, and so of the reality they aspire to disclose. And this perfectionist structure displays the internal relatedness of the concepts of authority, revelation, testimony, and the personal. For it is the nun's incarnation of her moral vision that not only reveals a whole new dimension of moral significance in human life but also authorizes it. The rightness of her vision is justified by the purity of her love; or more precisely, Gaita's impression of its purity rules out for him any speculation about whether it was justified. That is why he talks of being claimed in fidelity to her love: he has to speak personally because that is the nature of witness, and the only pertinent mode of authority or authorization here is that which attends an encounter with a particular other, the kind to which one can testify. And giving testimony invites, or rather compels, those to whom it is given either to testify to it in turn or to decline to do so. Each of his readers must judge whether Gaita's recounting of his encounter with this vision of goodness beyond virtue in the person of the nun is itself authoritative for him or her—something that claims us in fidelity to it, hence to him and to the nun.

Gaita himself is uncertain how much it matters that this authoritative individual was a nun; he talks of the work of saintly love, but acknowledges individuals who are not religious as undertaking it. Nevertheless, his work brings two distinctive features of Christianity into clearer focus. The first is the extent to which, as Helmut Gollwitzer puts it:

Biblical thinking remains true to the solid objectivity of the I–Thou relationship [which] is corroborated in its untranscendability and irreducibility by the experience of the divine encounter . . . in [terms of] the kinds of conduct that belong to the I–Thou relationship and can therefore be adequately expressed only in them . . . The kinds of conduct to which the biblical proclamation of God call us make sense only in relation to One who enters into the concrete mode of encounter between man and man and thereby enables these kinds of conduct as forms of relation to him: hearing, obeying, believing, loving, thanking, etc. (EG,[4] 156–7, 154)

Scriptural portrayals of God's dealings with men prefer particular and concrete ways of speaking over general and abstract ones, and the personal over the impersonal. But these preferences are authorized by Him, are His way of making it possible for us to relate to that which is absolutely Other to us, and so are not so much subsumable under the general category of person as revelatory of what personal relationships and personhood could and do really mean. This recalls the Thomist claim that the perfections apply to God, but do so more appropriately or fittingly than they do to us. For in giving expression to that semantic priority by knowingly violating the grammar of ordinary perfection talk (e.g. by saying that God is loving if and only if one says that he is Love), we maintain the appropriate theological balance between acknowledging scriptural authorization for characterizing our relations to God as personal whilst not characterizing God as a person (hence, as subsumable under categories, genus, and species). Gollwitzer again:

Personal terms like father and son, mother and child, lord and servant, friendship and the like become applicable to our relation to him, but he is not subjected to them i.e. the reference to him determines the application. In what sense he is Father, Lord, Friend etc. . . . can be ascertained only in view of his actions, not . . . by means of a rigid definition of these terms. The subject decides the predicate, not *vice versa*. (EG, 163)

The second distinctive feature of Christianity is its claim to fulfil the Old Testament phase of the Biblical tradition. For the doctrine of the Incarnation can then be seen as a radical perfecting of this incomprehensible but persistent sense of encounter with God as personal. Now God reveals Himself as an individual human being, one who claims that it is he to whom the perfections and the transcendentals fully and collectively apply (upon whom they incomprehensibly converge), and thereby reveals our prior understandings of them (both philosophical and Biblical) to be profoundly impoverished. Christ is not on the way, he is the Way; he is not asserting the truth, he is the Truth; he is not merely alive,

---

[4] *The Existence of God as Confessed by Faith*, trans. J. Leitch (London: SCM Press, 1965).

he is Life. Those who testify to his divinity proclaim the wholesale conversion process to which his life on earth subjects every one of our perfection terms—their radical redefinition and untranscendable fulfilment in relation to him; and they are claimed in fidelity to his every riddling, parabolic speech act as absolutely authoritative, divinely revelatory. One might say that, insofar as Christ is the enigmatic solution to the great riddle of life's meaning, then his fully divine and fully human status is not just analogous to the solution to the Sphinx's riddle (Diamond's analogous examplar): it *is* that solution. Christ reveals that the solution to the Sphinx's riddle ('human existence') is itself a riddle, and so too is the answer to *that* riddle. For that answer is not Oedipus or any of the morals that thinkers and poets have drawn from Oedipus' tragically transfigured life, but rather Christ himself.

6.3 Conclusion: The Temptation of Intelligibility

To conclude this investigation in the spirit in which it has been conducted, I want to offer not a summary of theses and hypotheses but a concrete, exemplary instance of religious encounter, theological elucidation, and philosophical appropriation in which all of the conceptual articulations I have been trying to disclose are perspicuously embodied: Kierkegaard's pseudonymous engagement (under the name of Johannes de Silentio) with the Old Testament tale of Abraham's willingness to sacrifice his son, Isaac (in *Fear and Trembling*[5]). For de Silentio, that tale hinges on two riddling utterances, and is itself a riddle that will only be solved (from a Christian point of view) by a further riddling revelation of the nature of the God whose relation with his chosen people is so decisively shaped by his shaping of this encounter with Abraham.

The first riddling utterance is God's:

And it came to pass after these things that God did tempt Abraham and said unto him... Take now thy son, thine only son Isaac, whom thou lovest, and get thee into the land of Moriah; and offer him there for a burnt offering upon one of the mountains which I will tell thee of. (Genesis, 22:1–2)

---

[5] Ed. and trans. H.V. Hong and E.H. Hong (Princeton, NJ: Princeton University Press, 1983), hereafter FT.

This utterance could have made perfect religious sense in its historical context: it fits one then-prevalent model of human relations to the gods, in which human sacrifice is a legitimate form of worship. However, this demand issues from a God who has already performed a miracle in bringing Isaac into existence, so as to make it possible to fulfil God's previous promise to make Abraham the father of many nations. How can Abraham make sense of his conviction that the author of this demand is also the author of that promise, and always speaks truly?

His solution is no less enigmatic than the riddle. When Isaac asks him what he intends to sacrifice, Abraham says: 'My son, God will provide himself a lamb for a burnt offering.' He proffers a form of words that will be made true by whatever he can imagine that God may allow or require on the mountain-top: either the sacrifice of his lamb, his beloved son, Isaac, who was after all a gift from God, or that of a substitute, a non-human animal of exactly the kind upon whose sacrifice God originally founded his covenant with Abraham (in Genesis 15), and over which God's earlier covenant with Noah gave humans dominion (in Genesis 9). In other words, Abraham attempts to project God's previous modes of action into the present context, so that his integrity and truthfulness are preserved (as is Abraham's relation to Isaac), without dispelling the darkness of his current intentions.

But it turns out that God's solution to his own riddle perfects Abraham's: for he creates a context into which Abraham's solution can be projected so as to make it true, but in a way that exceeds the range of possibilities Abraham could envisage. He provides a ram for the sacrifice, not a lamb. But this falsification of what Abraham literally said brings God's present action into line with his past actions (insofar as the founding covenantal sacrifice with Abraham involved a ram rather than a lamb); and it discloses Abraham's words as prophetically true—prefiguring a dimension of Christian significance that becomes available only through God's revelation of himself in Jesus Christ, and Christ's revelation of himself as the fulfilment of such earlier Biblical scenes, the divinely authorized solution to the riddles they pose. Christ is their beginning and their end, the perfecting or self-overcoming of the Abrahamic understanding of our relation to God. For the Incarnation reveals God as triune, his inner life exhibiting perfect Fatherhood and Sonhood insofar as Christ is revealed as the Lamb of God, the Son that the Heavenly Father provides for the sacrifice. And that revelation discloses

not only that our prior understanding of God was profoundly impoverished, but so too was our prior understanding of sacrifice (whose fullest
meaning is sacrifice of oneself), and so our understanding of love,
goodness, fatherhood, and sonhood, and so apparently endlessly on.

   If the solution to the riddle God sets or poses Abraham is Christ, then
two things follow. First, the insolubility of the riddle for and by Abraham
was necessary rather than contingent. The enigmatic quality of his
experience was internal to its nature, which any adequate expression of
that experience would have to acknowledge, and Abraham's utterance to
Isaac does so. For it presents the ultimate object of sacrifice as necessarily
being of divine—and so mysterious—origin (which in part means that it
riddlingly characterizes Isaac to himself as a gift whose origins are
mysterious); and it embodies a dimension of significance no more
accessible to the son than to the father. Second, if the solution is God
Incarnate, it is no less intrinsically enigmatic than the riddle it claims to
have solved.

   How might a philosophically sensitive Christian thinker, who understood Abraham's claim on us as a father of faith in these terms, awaken
such an understanding in his readers? Perhaps by constructing a pseudo-
nym whose way of presenting the Genesis narrative bears multiple
witness to the folly of presuming to understand it. So de Silentio insists
throughout that his authorial relation to Abraham is one of marvelling
incomprehension ('Abraham I cannot understand . . . I can learn nothing
from him except to be amazed' (FT, 37)); he exhibits his endlessly
renewed suffering of the offence to his understanding that this father
of faith exemplifies, in all its seductiveness. Moreover, he begins by
carefully distinguishing Abraham from other versions of himself, in the
Exordium's account of four counterfactual or pseudo-Abrahams whose
varying responses to God's demand resemble one another only insofar as
they conform to ordinary modes of psychological and moral explanation.
He thereby implies that Abraham is intrinsically elusive precisely
because he eludes those modes of explanation, and so may be best
delineated by repeatedly saying who and what he is not. Then he insists
that the assumed Christianity of his readers positively hinders us from
grasping Abraham, insofar as we think that Christianity has solved the
riddle Abraham confronts and represents—as if the New Testament
hands us a comprehensible answer to the riddle of maintaining one's
faith. We might, for example, make sense of Abraham by drawing an

edifying moral from this apparently barbarous tale (such as the smug pastor's 'we must be willing to offer God our best'), rather than allowing it to confront us with an impossible spiritual ideal (of unconditional dying to the self) and demanding our fidelity to it. Only far behind these nested textual barriers (in the 'Problemata') is Abraham directly portrayed as someone whose inability to make himself intelligible to others is a function of his incomprehensibility to himself, which results from his incomprehensible willingness to inhabit the ethically and rationally incomprehensible relation to his son that his relation to God demands.

Here, de Silentio notoriously emphasizes the extent to which Abraham is rooted in but ultimately outruns ethical understanding (instantiating 'a teleological suspension of the ethical'). Stanley Cavell registers the general shape of this discontinuous continuity in the following passage:

There are conflicts which can throw morality as a whole into question, but the significance of this question is not, or not necessarily, that the validity of morality is under suspicion, but perhaps that its competence as the judge of conduct and character is limited. This is what Kierkegaard meant by the 'teleological suspension of the ethical', and what Nietzsche means by defining a position 'beyond good and evil'. What they meant is that there is a position whose excellence we cannot deny, taken by persons we are not willing or able to dismiss, but which, *morally*, would have to be called wrong. And this has provided a major theme of modern literature: the salvation of the self through the repudiation of morality.

(CR, 269)

Cavell is here exploiting the dimension of ethical thinking that Gaita's work emphasizes—in which one's ethical understanding can be revolutionized by individuals whose example compels fidelity, calling us to bear witness, and so calling us out from the general ranks of ethical agency. So he emphasizes that such repudiations might be effected in a variety of ways—'by the prophet or the raging and suffering self, or by the delinquent or the oldest and newest evil'—*and* that 'not just anybody, in *any way*, can repudiate it' (CR, 269). Nietzsche's Zarathustra's way of going beyond good and evil is not for everyone; but then again, Zarathustra's way is not that of Anna Karenina or of Gauguin, nor that of Raskolnikov or Marx or de Sade. So how exactly does Abraham fit into this gallery of repudiators?

For the Anna Karenina and Paul Gauguin of Bernard Williams' fertile imagination, morality as such has become something to be repudiated, but only in the name of a species of excellence (whether that be romantic or artistic fulfilment) that can happily be incorporated within a broader vision of the ethical, conceived of as the task of living well or flourishing.[6] Here, morality's appeal is relativized, but only within the ethical. More precisely, morality is reconceived as one species of ethical value that can come into conflict with other such values and be trumped by them—overridden in ways that those concerned can justify to themselves and hope to render intelligible to others without expecting their agreement, and without needing to reconceive the trumped ethical values as somehow less than ethical.

De Silentio delineates this conflictual field by reference to such figures as Agamemnon—inhabitants of the domain of Greek tragic drama; and he aims to show thereby that Abraham, by contrast, relativizes the ethical as such. By relating absolutely to God, he relates relatively not only to a distinctively Kantian construal of ethics (as the morality system), but to values that any ethical being would regard as fundamental. For on de Silentio's account, to treat as absolute even the ethical prohibition against murder of the innocent, indeed of the innocent flesh of one's flesh, would be to succumb to temptation, to the appeal of something lower.

What is happening to the idea of 'temptation' in de Silentio's hands here should seem familiar. In everyday contexts, a temptation tempts us away from a specific ethical claim or demand: it is thus itself specific (a genus with a variety of species), as specific as the claim from which it aims to turn us away (any such claim being a species of the ethical genus). Temptation thus reveals ethical claims as being just as concrete, conditioned, and context-relative—just as much dependent for their content and force upon logical ties to their surroundings—as the temptations they set their face against. One might therefore say that the ethical as such is a domain of relative value; hence to relate oneself relatively to ethical value is simply to relate to such value as it really is. If one should only relate absolutely to that which is of absolute value, then one should not relate absolutely to the ethical. One might even say (with another of Kierkegaard's pseudonyms, Johannes Climacus) that to relate absolutely to what is of absolute value *just is* to relate relatively to that which is of relative value. Relating relatively to the relative is how one's absolute relation to the absolute makes itself manifest, is in fact all that it can amount to (logically speaking).

---

[6] Cf. the title essay of his *Moral Luck* (Cambridge: Cambridge University Press, 1981).

But if one characterizes the ethical as such as a temptation, the concept of a temptation is now not relative or specific but absolute or unconditioned. De Silentio is saying that, no matter what ethical claim we are concerned with and how it bears upon the circumstances of our lives, from the perspective of a father of faith it is capable of constituting a temptation. Now, ethical value can appear as unconditionally or absolutely a source of temptation only in the light of a conception of absolute value according to which all relatively valuable claims on us appear indistinguishably or unconditionally lower. But if this realm of value is absolutely higher, then what its value consists in cannot be accounted for; this is because its being absolute just is a matter of its logical ties to context and circumstance being absolutely severed. To construct such a concept is thus to bring oneself up against the limits of the intelligible, the limits of thought and language. In this respect, the violence that de Silentio does to the concept of a temptation mirrors the violence he does to the notion of value. An evaluative term that is essentially tied to its specific contexts of use is stripped of those ties and clung to as a more perfect expression of value (not despite the fact that, but precisely because) the operation that produced it deprives it of sense.

The echo of the early Wittgenstein's conception of the relation between relative and absolute judgements of value is, I hope, clear; and it returns us to the idea of Judaeo-Christian religion's way of resisting assignments of sense. For de Silentio's point is not simply that Abraham will seem unintelligible to those who relate absolutely to the ethical—as if implying that we can make sense of him if only we can find the right (the appropriately religious) mode of discourse in which to do so. It is that Abraham's God-relation can only find appropriate expression in his *not* making sense, in his resisting any attempts to assign sense to the words to which he clings. The only way of making sense of Abraham is to grasp the point of his not making sense—to see him as having a very particular use for a very specifically generated kind of nonsense.

My suggestion, then, is that our relation to Abraham constitutes (because Abraham's relation to God constitutes) what Cora Diamond has called 'a difficulty of reality':

[T]he phenomena with which I'm concerned [are] experiences in which we take something in reality to be resistant to our thinking it, or possibly to be painful in its inexplicability, difficult in that way, or perhaps awesome and astonishing in its inexplicability. *We take things so.* And the things we take so may simply not, to others, present that kind of difficulty, of being hard or impossible or agonizing to get one's mind around. (DR,[7] 99)

I mentioned such resistance to the understanding in Lecture Two, when we examined the early Wittgenstein's view of absolute value; and many of Diamond's other examples of the phenomenon are also ethico-aesthetic. They include J.M. Coetzee's fictional protagonist Elizabeth Costello (with her maddened, isolating perception of the moral barbarism of our treatment of non-human animals); Czesław Miłosz' talk of beauty (the architecture of a tree, the dawn chorus) as something that should not exist, for which there are no reasons for and indeed reasons against, but which nevertheless undoubtedly exist; and Roy Holland's conception of the miraculous as the occurrence of something which is empirically certain and conceptually impossible.[8] Many philosophers would rule out any such 'conception' in advance, because it violates the very idea of a conceptual order in the absence of which the possibility of genuine thought will vanish. Others may be willing to take seriously the possibility that one's experience might force one to violate one's idea of what a well-ordered concept, and so well-ordered thinking, must be.

A difficulty of reality, then, is an apparent resistance by reality to one's ordinary modes of life, which include one's ordinary modes of thinking and talking; to appreciate that kind of difficulty 'is to appreciate oneself being shouldered out of how one thinks, how one is apparently supposed to think' (DR, 105). Recast in Wittgensteinian terms, such phenomena ask us to acknowledge the capacity of reality to shoulder us out from our familiar language-games, to resist the distinctively human capacity to word the world, and thereby to leave us as bewildered and disoriented as a bird that suddenly finds itself incapable of constructing a nest, or a beaver of building a dam. It could only mislead to say that being shouldered out of our language-games is just one more language-game, or to declare that words have a grammar when they fail us just as they do when we effortlessly employ them to word the world. Indeed, it would amount to failing to register philosophically the kind of difficulty that difficulties of reality pose—failing to register that they resist the grammar of Wittgensteinian terms such as 'language-game', 'grammar', and 'form

---

[7] In 'The Difficulty of Reality and the Difficulty of Philosophy', in A. Crary and S. Shieh (eds), *Reading Cavell* (London: Routledge, 2006), hereafter DR.

[8] 'The Miraculous', in his *Against Empiricism* (Totowa, NJ: Barnes and Noble, 1980).

of life' just as radically as they resist that of any other aspects of our thinking and talking.

Cast in theological terms, one might say (with Kathryn Tanner) that 'God becomes the . . . paradigm for all that remains indigestible to sense-making practices that insist on the exhaustive, homogenizing subsumption of particulars under general concepts . . . the model for resistance to the Same' (CEMM,[9] p 139). The 'grammatical' circle theology draws around philosophy thus testifies to a sense of reality as inherently capable of utterly bewildering our abilities to make sense of it, with the sheer wild particularity (Aquinas might call it the *esse*) of each individual thing harbouring a refusal to conform to or be exhausted by any of our orderings of things.

Here Diamond, Wittgenstein, and Aquinas make contact with Chesterton's ethics of elfland—the vision of reality that he acquired from fairy tales. Central to that vision is the conviction that the only locus of genuine necessity is the orderings of mathematics and logic. To think that actual things exhibit such necessity—to think that the fact that trees bear fruit is just as necessary as the fact that one and two trees make three—is to conflate the distinction between a true law and mere fact:

A law implies that we know the nature of the generalisation and enactment; not merely that we have noticed some of the effects. . . . [But] we cannot say why an egg can turn into a chicken any more than we could say why a bear could turn into a fairy prince. As *ideas*, the egg and the chicken are further off from each other than the bear and the prince; for no egg in itself suggests a chicken, whereas some princes do suggest bears. Granted, then, that certain transformations do happen, it is essential that we should regard them in the philosophical manner of fairy tales, not in the unphilosophic manner of science . . . When we are asked why eggs turn into birds or fruit falls in the autumn, we must answer exactly as the fairy godmother would answer if Cinderella asked her why mice turned to horses or her clothes fell from her at twelve o'clock. We must answer that it is *magic*. It is not a law, for we do not understand its general formula. It is not a necessity, for though we can count on it happening practically, we have no right to say that it must always happen . . . We leave [the possibility of a miracle] out of account, not because it is a miracle and therefore an impossibility, but because it is a miracle and therefore an exception. . . . The only words that ever satisfied me as describing Nature are the terms used in the fairy books, 'charm', 'spell', 'enchantment'. They express the arbitrariness of the fact, and its mystery.

---

[9] 'Creation *Ex Nihilo* as Mixed Metaphor', in J. Soskice (ed.), *Creation 'Ex Nihilo' and Modern Theology* (Oxford: Blackwell, 2013).

A tree grows fruit because it is a *magic* tree. Water runs downhill because it is bewitched. The sun shines because it is bewitched. (O,[10] 69–70)

If we discount the (perhaps unduly) Humean vehicle of Chesterton's vision, its spirit might well seem complementary to that of Wittgenstein's notorious expression of scepticism about the Laws of Nature, in his notes on cause and effect.

Think of two different kinds of plant, A and B, both of which yield seeds. The seeds of both kinds look exactly the same and even after the most careful investigation we can find no difference between them. But the seeds of an A-plant always produce more A-plants, the seeds of a B-plant more B-plants...

And to protest 'There *must* be a difference in the seeds, even if we don't discover it' doesn't alter the facts, it only shows what a powerful urge we have to see everything in terms of cause and effect. (NCE,[11] 373–5)

Whatever one makes of this analogy, the crucial point in the present context is that the paradigm case of the wild particularity or enigmatic resistance of reality to which all these thinkers are referring is that of the human individual and his forms of life.

This is why de Silentio presents Abraham as finding himself shouldered out of our language-games of ethical value. He cannot keep faith with his experience except by resisting any attempt to make sense of it in the terms provided by those language-games. This means that he must regard these available modes of intelligibility as a standing temptation to lose faith with the absolute, which in turn amounts to regarding resistance to explication (keeping reason unseated or unhorsed) as constitutive of the unconditionally valuable. To inhabit such a sphere of existence or form of life is thus to confront a difficulty of reality without any prospect of overcoming it. Such individuals must rather bear witness to it precisely as resistant to comprehension, and so must anyone (such as de Silentio) who finds himself claimed in fidelity by such individuals. But of course, what one individual sees as undeniably but incomprehensibly significant may be seen by others as utterly empty—something that, if it is not reducible to the everyday, can only be a mere illusion of transcendence.

Difficulties of reality will thereby tend to isolate individuals, disclosing others as opaque to them and themselves as opaque to those others.

---

[10]   G.K. Chesterton, *Orthodoxy* (London: Hodder and Stoughton, 1999/1908).
[11]   'Notes on Cause and Effect', in J.C. Klagge and A. Nordmann (eds), *Wittgenstein: Philosophical Occasions* (Indianapolis: Hackett, 1993).

Anyone bearing witness to reality's resistance to her understanding thereby resists our understanding, and so reveals all of us as essentially capable of resisting one another's understanding. Hence, relating to the absolutely good as mysterious entails acknowledging those who attempt to realize such a relation as mysterious. The otherness of other people, and so their reality to us as our others, is partly determined by the fact that we can be injuriously incomprehensible to one another—that what one of us finds wounding to the point of madness the other finds to be empty, and that abyss of incomprehension itself deepens the wound to which the other is utterly oblivious.

How much easier it would be to live with such maddened and maddening others if we could deflect the existential challenge they present— that of making human sense of their resistance to our ordinary ways of making sense of things, and of one another—into an intellectual problem. But could philosophy deflect itself from such temptations to deflect, and still know itself? Suppose philosophy acknowledged theology as bearing witness to reality's capacity to outrun our modes of reflective appraisal. Then it would necessarily either be claimed in fidelity to that testimony or bound to reject it; and it would know that if it chooses rejection, it would be in the name of its own defining wager that sense can be always be made of the diverse unity of our practices of sense-making. It would, in short, be forced to acknowledge that this rejection is no more, and of course no less, than an expression of faith in itself.

Epilogue

Although I knew that Rowan Williams had been delivering his Gifford Lectures a few months before I gave my own, it was only after I completed revisions to this manuscript that those lectures were published,[1] and I discovered how far his explorations seem consonant with my own—particularly with respect to his opening readings of Aquinas and his repeated recourse to Cavell, but also in his more general concern with analogical speech and thought, and with varieties of what he calls 'extreme' utterance. I would have liked to discuss these points of resemblance (and so of contrast) in more detail here, but for my suspicion that doing so would require something closer to a book-length work, or the reworking of every chapter in this book. Besides, another way of bringing this book to a briefer and more manageable conclusion had already presented itself.

A few weeks after delivering these lectures, I came across a book by Adam Roberts—professor of nineteenth century literature at Royal Holloway, University of London, and noted science fiction author—entitled *The Riddles of* The Hobbit.[2] The core concern of the book is to contest the widely shared belief that *The Hobbit* is a lesser work than *The Lord of the Rings*, primarily by demonstrating that Tolkien's book for children has an interest in, and a sense of the significance of, riddles and riddling that extends far beyond the famous chapter in which Bilbo escapes from Gollum (unscathed, and in possession of the famous ring) by besting him in a riddle contest. What interested me most, however, was the way in which Roberts connects the *topos* of the riddle with a complex nesting of broader contexts which both reinforce and extend some of the conjunctions I have been attempting to establish and explore in this set of lectures. So it would seem churlish—a display of unhappy ingratitude

---

[1] *The Edge of Words: God and the Habits of Language* (London: Bloomsbury, 2014).
[2] (London: Palgrave Macmillan, 2013), hereafter RH.

at an unlooked-for gift—to depart from the scene without at least laying out the disconcerting extent of the convergence of Roberts' assumptions with my own.

Roberts introduces his argument by relating riddles to literature, Anglo-Saxon (and more generally Northern European) culture, and religion. With respect to literature, he claims that riddling is not only a very minor literary genre on its own: it is also a textual strategy that is vital to poetry, and a figure for the business of reading or interpretation—call it hermeneutics—more generally. He predictably cites Metaphysical and Martian poetry as modes that explicitly foreground riddling conceits: Donne asks 'How is love like the two limbs of a divider?', and Raine asks 'How is memory like an onion?' (his answer is not 'because it is layered', or 'because it grows as it is buried', but rather 'because it makes me cry'). But Roberts also argues that such conceits are a familiar aspect of a far broader range of poetic composition (including work by Kipling, Graves, and Auden), and then articulates an inclination to claim that 'any poem requires a sort of unriddling, even if it is merely the construction of a context that makes sense of the direct' (RH, 10).

He notes the obvious objection—that this dilutes the meaning of the word 'riddling' to the point where it loses any purchase; but he points out that such an argument assumes that the task enunciated is simple and easily carried out—that most poetry can be straightforwardly decoded, and that what the decoded version points us towards is itself simple and easily grasped. Roberts' view, by contrast, is that locating the context within which all of a poem's direct articulations make sense is typically a complex exercise of right judgement from case to case; and that once reached, the relevant solutions take us to phenomena—such as memory or love—that are very far from simple, and indeed whose lack of perspicuity is very often precisely what preoccupied the poet.

Such literary art stands in a relationship to reality which is ironic rather than mimetic (I would rather be inclined to say that it assumes that aspiring to a genuine mimesis of reality very often requires the establishment of an ironic relation to it):

[M]ore a process of opening disclosure than a narrowing-down enclosure . . . [I]t is only familiarity that stands between us and a vision of the world as a fascinating but baffling series of puzzles to be decoded . . . [I]f the doors of perception were cleansed to a properly Martian cleanliness we should see the world as it truly is, *a riddle*. (RH, 13–14)

It is this kind of world view that scholars take to lie at the roots of pre-Conquest Anglo-Saxon culture of the kind in which Tolkien was so deeply interested. Roberts quotes a scholar of the period claiming that 'poetical riddles were produced in England more largely than anywhere else in the Dark Ages, both in Latin and the native tongue' (RH, 7); and he claims that this bespeaks a fascination on their part with the relationship between the structure of language and the structure of the cosmos. In other words, riddles speak to the puzzling circumstances in which these people found themselves—call it the human condition:

Riddles are a truer representation of the nature of reality than simple declarative statements. This is because . . . the world is not a simple or transparent business, but a mystery to be plumbed. Riddles . . . talk about ordinary objects or phenomena in an ironic way: sly, allusive, misleading . . .

This speaks in the largest way to the way the Old Northmen lived their lives. Irony is a way of expressing a sense that there is a gap between oneself and one's world, a mismatch between will and thing . . . Take, for example, death. The Old English approach to this existential universal was a grim sort of acceptance that we must inevitably die, combined with a wry sense of the ironic mismatch [with] how much life we have in our doomed hearts . . . Their gods were capricious, puzzling creatures because life is often that way; and those same Norse gods were themselves doomed to die . . . because human life is so doomed. The question as to why that is poses one of the most profound riddles of all. (RH, 20)

Here, Roberts sees a connection between Tolkien's interest in Anglo-Saxon culture and his Catholicism; and I need only present a bouquet of his remarks on this latter context in order to demonstrate its extensive affinities with my own preoccupations (my occasional interpolated remarks in curly brackets underline the less evident ones):

Religious mysteries are, in a strict sense, riddles. That might look like a trivializing way of talking about faith, but I prefer to think about it the other way around—as a way of elevating the significance and dignity of riddles . . . . [R]iddles embody in a small way a very large observation about human existence. Life riddles us. (RH, 2)

[St] Paul says: existence is a riddle of which the solution has been unknown, until now. The solution he proposes is, in a word, Christ. But this answer folds back on itself in that the answer to this riddle is itself a riddle, what Paul calls 'the mystery of Christ'. (RH, 3)

We need to take Tolkien's cordial dislike of allegory seriously . . . On one level, he is making a fundamentally religious point. For a Christian, Christ is not a 'symbol' of God; he does not . . . *allegorically represent* God in the mortal realm. Christ *is* God, incarnated in human form . . . C.S. Lewis' Aslan does not *allegorise*

Christ; he is the form Christ's incarnation would take in a world of talking animals {Burrell might call him an analogous projection of Christ into Narnia}. (RH, 12)

[A] riddle, formally speaking, is a small example of something unseen presenting itself to us and asking to be seen. It is, as it were, a thing wearing a ring of invisibility. Our wits are the mode by which it can be made visible again. 'Blessed are the eyes', Christ told his disciples, 'which see the things which ye see. For I tell you, that many prophets and kings have desired to see those things which ye see, and have not seen them' (Luke, 10:23). (RH, 13)

[Seeing] the world as it truly is, *a riddle* . . . connects with the larger sense {shared by Gollwitzer} that human subjectivity—mind, personality, soul—is itself a riddle . . . [O]ne of Freud's key insights [is] that . . . our self-knowledge is an ironic business, slant, full of obscurity and gaps . . . we are a riddle unto ourselves and [he] sets up psychoanalysis as a means of unriddling the puzzle of psychosis, trauma, hysteria, or plain old human unhappiness. A dream . . . is a riddle to be decoded with access to the right sort of reading competencies. (RH, 14)

One of the ways the unexamined wisdom of children manifests itself in the world, one of the ways in which the child *is* father to the man, is the way kids ask riddles all the time: why is the sky blue? Why is water wet? Why is that man crying? Why are that woman and that man cuddling so close? . . . 'Why is the sky blue' is more than a question . . . It is a way of reaching out towards the way beauty and wonder overroof our mundane worlds. It is to take the step beyond merely registering the glory of a blue sky, into the realm of wanting to comprehend that glory. It is, that is to say, intensely human. {It is also intensely Heideggerian, and Chestertonian.} (RH, 15)

Perhaps my sense of uncanny intimacy, of being repeatedly and (in essentials) accurately spoken for, here is merely the reflection of the fact that I was brought up as a Catholic in the north-east of England, and was immersed in Tolkien as an adolescent. Even so, I am tempted to say: the spirit of Roberts' book exhibits the form that Grammatical Thomism would take in the world of literary criticism.

Bibliography

Aquinas, T., *Summa Theologiae: Questions on God*, ed. Davies, B. and Leftow. B. (Cambridge: Cambridge University Press, 2006).

Burrell, D., *Analogy and Philosophical Language* (New Haven, CT: Yale University Press, 1973).

Burrell, D., *Aquinas: God and Action* (London: Routledge and Kegan Paul, 1979).

Cavell, S., 'Declining Decline', in S. Mulhall (ed.), *The Cavell Reader* (Oxford: Blackwell, 1996).

Cavell, S., *The Claim of Reason* (Oxford: Oxford University Press, 1979; new edition 1999).

Chesterton, G.K., *Orthodoxy* (London: Hodder and Stoughton, 1999/1908).

Conant, J., 'The Method of the *Tractatus*', in E. Reck (ed.), *From Frege to Wittgenstein* (Oxford: Oxford University Press, 2002).

Conant, J. and Diamond, C., 'On Reading the *Tractatus* Resolutely', in M. Kölbel and B. Weiss (eds), *Wittgenstein's Lasting Significance* (London: Routledge, 2004).

Diamond, C., *The Realistic Spirit* (Cambridge: MIT Press, 1991).

Diamond, C., 'Ethics, Imagination and the Method of the *Tractatus*', in A. Crary and R. Read (eds), *The New Wittgenstein* (London: Routledge, 2000).

Diamond, C., 'Wittgenstein and Religious Belief: The Gulfs between Us', in D.Z. Phillips and M. von der Ruhr (eds), *Religion and Wittgenstein's Legacy* (London: Ashgate, 2005).

Diamond, C., 'The Difficulty of Reality and the Difficulty of Philosophy', in A. Crary and S. Shieh (eds), *Reading Cavell* (London: Routledge, 2006).

Gaita, R., *A Common Humanity* (London: Routledge, 2000).

Gollwitzer, H., *The Existence of God as Confessed by Faith*, trans. J. Leitch (London: SCM Press, 1965).

Hacker, P.M.S., *Wittgenstein: Understanding and Meaning*, parts I and II (Oxford: Blackwell, 2005).

Heidegger, M., *Being and Time*, trans. J. MacQuarrie and E. Robinson (Oxford: Blackwell, 1962).

Holland, R., 'The Miraculous', in *Against Empiricism* (Totowa, NJ: Barnes and Noble, 1980).

Kant, I., *Critique of the Power of Judgement*, trans. P. Guyer and E. Matthews (Cambridge: Cambridge University Press, 2001).

Kenny, A., *The Five Ways* (London: Routledge and Kegan Paul, 1969).

Kierkegaard, S., *The Journals*, ed. A. Dru (Oxford: Oxford University Press, 1938).

Kierkegaard, S., *Fear and Trembling*, ed. and trans. H.V. Hong and E.H. Hong (Princeton, NJ: Princeton University Press, 1983).

Kierkegaard, S., *Concluding Unscientific Postscript*, ed. and trans. H.V. Hong and E.H. Hong (Princeton, NJ: Princeton University Press, 1992).

Malcolm, N., 'Anselm's Ontological Arguments', in *Knowledge and Certainty* (Englewood Cliffs, NJ: Prentice-Hall, 1963).

McCabe, H., 'Creation', in *God Matters* (London: Geoffrey Chapman, 1987).

McCabe, H., Appendices 2 and 3, *Summa Theologiae*, vol. 3 (1a. 12–13), *Knowing and Naming God*, trans. H. McCabe (Cambridge: Cambridge University Press, 2006).

Mulhall, S., *Inheritance and Originality* (Oxford: Oxford University Press, 2001).

Mulhall, S., 'Wittgenstein on Religious Belief', in O. Kuusela and M. McGinn (eds), *The Oxford Handbook of Wittgenstein* (Oxford: Oxford University Press, 2012).

Murphy, F. Aran, *God is Not a Story* (Oxford: Oxford University Press, 2007).

Nielsen, K., 'Wittgensteinian Fideism', in K. Nielsen and D.Z. Phillips (eds), *Wittgensteinian Fideism* (London: SCM Press, 2005).

Phillips, D.Z., *Faith after Foundationalism* (London: Routledge, 1989).

Phillips, D.Z., *Wittgenstein and Religion* (London: Routledge, 1993).

Preller, V., *Divine Science and the Science of God: A Reformulation of Thomas Aquinas* (Princeton, NJ: Princeton University Press, 1967).

Roberts, A., *The Riddles of* The Hobbit (London: Palgrave Macmillan, 2013).

Rundle, B., *Wittgenstein and Contemporary Philosophy of Language* (Oxford: Blackwell, 1990).

Rundle, B., *Why there is Something rather than Nothing* (Oxford: Oxford University Press, 2004).

Stout, J. and MacSwain, R. (eds), *Grammar and Grace: Reformulations of Aquinas and Wittgenstein* (London: SCM Press, 1984).

Tanner, K., 'Creation *Ex Nihilo* as Mixed Metaphor', in J. Soskice (ed.), *Creation 'Ex Nihilo' and Modern Theology* (Oxford: Blackwell, 2013).

Turner, D., *The Darkness of God* (Cambridge: Cambridge University Press, 1995).

Turner, D., *Faith, Reason and the Existence of God* (Cambridge: Cambridge University Press, 2004).

White, R.M., *Talking About God* (Farnham: Ashgate, 2010).

Williams, B., *Moral Luck* (Cambridge: Cambridge University Press, 1981).

Williams, R., *The Edge of Words: God and the Habits of Language* (London: Bloomsbury, 2014).

Wittgenstein, L., *Tractatus Logico-Philosophicus* (London: Routledge and Kegan Paul, 1922).

Wittgenstein, *Lectures on the Foundations of Mathematics, Cambridge 1939*, ed. C. Diamond (Chicago: University of Chicago Press, 1989).

Wittgenstein, L., 'Lecture on Ethics', in J.C. Klagge and A. Nordmann (eds), *Wittgenstein: Philosophical Occasions* (Indianapolis: Hackett, 1993).

Wittgenstein, L., 'Notes on Cause and Effect', in J.C. Klagge and A. Nordmann (eds), *Wittgenstein: Philosophical Occasions* (Indianapolis: Hackett, 1993).

Wittgenstein, L., *Philosophical Investigations*, 4th edition, trans. Anscombe, Hacker, and Schulte, ed. Hacker and Schulte (Oxford: Blackwell, 2009).

Index